Markings

26

Published by Markings Publications

THE BAKEHOUSE

The Bakehouse
44 High Street
Gatehouse of Fleet
DG7 2HP Scotland
www.markings.org.uk

with assistance from

Scottish
Arts Council

Dumfries
& Galloway
C O U N C I L

BDS

BIBLIOGRAPHIC DATA SERVICES

ISSN 1460-7166
ISBN 9781901913 05 7

Lead editor: John Hudson
Editors: Elspeth Brown & Chrys Salt
Design & layout: John Hudson
Tel: +44131 208 3534 Mob: +447801801204
Email info@markings.org.uk

Cover image © Ailsa Black, opposite Gail Kelly

CONTENTS

Fiction

Features

Reviews   112

Art

Gail Kelly

Ailsa Black

Note for contributors

Markings gladly considers unsolicited submissions of poetry, fiction, artwork and criticism.

Please forward work to submissions@markings.org.uk in electronic format, preferably using Microsoft Word or saved as rich text or plain text in other word processors. Please keep formatting to a minimum and avoid, where possible, use of tabs, fully capitalised titles, multiple spaces, underscores as these will need to be taken out or replaced with the house style. This will best ensure that your wishes with regard to appearance are maintained in the type-setting process.

Artwork is best sent in greyscale jpg format, minimum 200 dpi.

When sending by post enclose an SSAE with the correct postage to the address on the title page verso. Please mark all pages clearly with your name and address and include an email address and telephone number if possible.

Should you require a proof before going to press please ensure that you have an email address and a pdf reader.

Issue 26 of Markings changes shape

Physically, stylistically and in its editorial make-up, Markings has changed. Our new larger format allows us to get that bit more breathing space for our contributors' work and it also enables us to undertake the first major typographical changes since Markings' inception in 1995. Out goes our long-serving Venetian type-face and in comes the bolder Bodoni. Why? Some readers have commented on the difficulty of reading Venetian, especially on the higher quality paper that Markings is now printed on. I have to agree. Perhaps it's the fact that I was 37 years' old when I started Markings and my eyesight then was much better than it is today – and I still refuse to wear glasses.

Another change is the departure from the Markings team of Elspeth Brown who helped Donald Adamson, Jeff White, Anne Darling, Tony Bonning and myself establish the magazine all those years ago. Elspeth leaves to devote more time to her own writing. She has been a loyal friend and colleague, a tireless worker for the Markings' cause and always great fun to be with. Elspeth edited the short stories, typed them up (in the days before e-copy was common), proof-read the magazine, did her fair share of admin and distributed the magazine in the east of Dumfries and Galloway and in Edinburgh. Just as importantly, she was a great ambassador for the magazine and the writers contained within it. Not only should we, the current editors, be grateful to her but all those who have been published in Markings owe her a big vote of thanks. We wish her well with her writing and look forward to reading her new work and in meeting up at The Bakehouse from time to time.

This issue devotes a section to the work of Elspeth Brown, and also to another champion of Scottish literature and of good writing in general. John Pick should need little introduction but his modesty possibly means that he might – at least to some. In the section devoted to him, which includes poetry, a short story and a critical essay, there are tributes from figures such as Professor Alan Riach, Tessa Ransford, Professor Roderick Watson and Stewart Conn. These and the quality of John's work will go a little way, we hope, to acknowledging and saying thank you for his contribution over the years.

Finally thank you all, writers, readers, editors and funders for supporting Markings. We are stocked in every library service in the country; our Literature in Libraries programme is discovering new talent and our allied performance space, The Bakehouse has even managed to get Shakespeare's Globe theatre to bring Romeo and Juliet to Dumfries.

Now Shakespeare... there's a talent Markings would have liked to have discovered...

John Hudson, Castle Douglas, April 2008

Plasma Nights

seductive bright light
        of the evening narrative

ease of habit
        the need to relax

heck
        we all need a break

so it goes
        day into night

something to talk about
        social cohesion

*

which is entertainment
        which is value

which is passing time
        which is bonding

movement on the retina
        movement in the brain

reinforcement
        which is

processed information
        spectator dialogue

plasma brother

      *

privileged
        by bombs
        we occupy

the dominant narrative

for subjects

far away
who may envy us

if seen
on their screen

Tom Leonard will be reading at The Bakehouse on June 28

Nuyoktok: 10 hours

1
Sometimes in summer it rains like this:
A dirty blind drops down mid-day.
We gasp. A glass tips over.

2
Oranges peaches garbage pulse.
x and x and x
siren   salsa

3
To be here and now in this place that's always starting
again, where buildings go up, come down, go up again,
with the frequency of a cartoon disaster where nothing
is constant. Nothing is fixed.

4
Here comes
the Halleluja man.
Wild wild ecstatic rhythms/ribbons
swoop and sign the street.

Halleluja! Halleluja! Halleluja!

3
This is the breath of cities.

4
The woman on the bus
could hardly care less who overhears:
So I said to him,
no point in wasting time.
I like you, I like your furniture.
How about we make it permanent?

5
Well, *that's* a good-looking poem, Bob says.

6
But what are people throwing out these days?
Styrofoam mattresses?
Stripped cans of Starkist Tuna?
A baby chair with Superman peeling.

7
I've got $41.76 and a phonecard good for long distance.

I leave the milk out on the counter.
It turns homesick in an hour.

8
Mid-afternoon, the same heat
stopped in the same acacia trees.
The same mad cicadas pedal furiously
on their rickety cicada bicycles

9
Shaka shaka shaka shaka

10
"Keep faith with the people."

"Somebody loves you."

"All vehicles subject to search."

RAYMOND FRIEL

Songs of the Plough
for Richard Price

Received out of darkness
into beery hubbub,
we dunted pint glasses,
looked round for a plum seat.
Work behind us, we'd do
whatever we liked now
(if what we *ought* to do
didn't come and join us,
like a difficult friend).
Snug there in Bloomsbury,
we sipped our good fortune -
in the homes we hirpled
back to (never *that* late),
in the poets we knew,
in our friendship that sprung
from nice-but-no letters
from *Gairfish*, to poring
over tumbler-circled
poems which winced under
your quick, critical eye;
in all that we loved from
Vermeer to the Blue Nile,
to the Soho restaurants
like Ming's in Greek Street,
where you boozily launched
Second Cities—Donny's
juiced Chicago postcards.

The high-stooled regulars
flirted with the barmaids
who were 'doing the UK'.
The quiz machine scrolled up
its pop culture teasers,
bleeping with smugness
at its store of knowledge.
What bothered us—our drunk
who wanted to talk—was
being 'a Scot' in England,
émigrés, not exiles,
in England's crucible
of the *un*privileged.
Some nights we improvised
a music hall routine,
cranking it up at 'time'
as Donald and Donald,
hamming up the accents
and off-the-trainisms,
daring the soft southerners
to boo us off the stage.

*The Plough—a pub near the British Museum in London once frequented by
Hugh MacDiarmid; Gairfish—a literary magazine; Second Cities—a collection
of poems by Donny O'Rourke*

Other nights, over tired -
peeved at reputations,
New Gen and their ad men,
rehearsing fantasies
of more quality time
in the public sector
circus we performed in
(or, gorged on house red
and Veneziana
in next door's pizza place,
indulging the baser
fantasies that waken
beneath blue-veined marble...)
On good nights, though, most nights,
after your sharp blether
the kind of poetry
I wanted (He bevvied
in this very howf,
all frizzy with genius...)
had raised its eyes beyond
the jist of what went on.

Postscript

For Katie's fifth birthday
you drove down to see us
in our Somerset nest.
After a pell-mell lunch
of weans and too much wine
we angled for an hour
for lit business, smuggled
neat drams with the bundles
of others' work to be
scrutinised for the mag
we laboured at awhile...
Belle and Sebastian
was your mellowing choice
of disc; mine *A Handful
of Earth*—(we need voices
we can actually *trust...*).

We were a decade on
from the spic-and-span boys
who worried over who
we were away from home.
Children and work, and time,
had loosened those concerns,
(cranked up plenty new ones...).
Years practising the art
on the side may have made us
better artists, but not
necessarily
better people—Auden
got that one about right.
So we're left with the cost -
and that's our business.

Ross Wilson

The Working Days

Money drives us together, and we
drive one another mad.
        But today, on our break, we had
a break from the usual back stabbing gossip
when the friend of a workmate
        died suddenly in a car crash,
early this morning.
        Shocked, we offered
well meaning clichés for condolence,
every last one well stocked
in our heads, like the responses we have
to many things now:
        Religion: *start of all wars* . . .
        Poetry: *crap* . . .
Like taps turned tight in the grip
of the times we're in,
our heads are turned off old ideas,
while our mouths drip monotonous refrains:
        It's just as well we don't know
        what's ahead of us.
More than one of us said that today.
It was a relief to go back to work again,
        chairs scraping away
from where we sat together.
        Alone, we sweated, groaned,
bitched behind backs, and moaned
about this, that, whatever;
        each of us wishing the day over.

And tomorrow.
      And the next day.
             And so on.
      I can't wait 'til Friday!
'*I*' being *we*, regardless of who said it
today,
      this time last week, or
             the week before.
Mid week, every week, we drop pounds
into a plastic money bag:
      pennies in a wishing well
on a table in the room where we change.
      It carries each of our names in biro,
letting us know who has paid
for what might come our way.
      For, as we say,
we don't know what's ahead of us, but
      the working days
that bring us together, and
      pull us apart.

GAIL KELLY

Japanese Garden

Rosemary Baker

A Bonsai Culture

Friday. Richard Nakomoto puts his pruning knife into his pocket. From the striped shade of a slatted canopy he surveys his garden. He thinks of his Father, Yuuki Nakomoto, who built this wooden shelter for his ancient bonsai, and of his Grandfather, Yoshi Nakomoto, who designed the garden. He bows. The sounds of bees and birds about their lawful business assure him that all is well.

After a while he eases his cotton trousers over his knees and sinks cross legged on to the weathered staging. His whole being settles slowly into the attitude of the lotus. His eyes close against light reflected from venerable rocks. Stressful illusions drain away and on the outstretched hand of the Buddha he floats into reality.

But fate intrudes. Presumptuous footsteps sound on stone: leather sandals striding heel-toe, heel-toe, get louder without humility: determined, wayward footsteps. A headstrong woman is beating a path into his sanctuary.

An illusion of pain grips his shoulder and the hand of the Buddha hardens to wooden planking beneath his thin haunches. The canopy still enfolds him in striped shade but the sunlit world materialises before him in brazen focus. Breathing systematically he takes conscious guard against anger. His Friday preparation for martial arts is interrupted, but he has no intention of losing control to demons, even in this aberrant situation.

A certain dissatisfaction has, of late, crept into the tenor of his English days and he has begun to cultivate a more formal Japanese disposition. Particularly he has dedicated his Friday evenings to practice with the Samurai sword. In keeping with his new devotion he has recently sacrificed an unruly bed of wind-blown Japanese anemones to make room for a courtyard of raked gravel.

He knows the approaching woman to be his sister-in-law. She assails the fortifications of his existence every time his wife goes into hospital to add to his family. At such times this relation-by-marriage becomes the custodian of his domestic establishment and, as such, she is a necessary evil. Just now she is bringing his lunch in a basket because she wants it out of her way. He would have preferred the table set waiting for him to go in. His

19

habit is to wash and change before his meal. She should clear away afterwards. It is hard to grasp that she and his wife are sisters. He has been wise in his choice.

Janet appears before him on the flagstones, a tall, angular figure in a limp cotton dress and big, flat sandals. She obliterates his view of the raked gravel and looks him in the eye. Before he has time to acknowledge her presence the woman speaks. "I've the shopping to do. You've let your freezer get almost empty so I've defrosted and washed it out. When you go in rinse your flask, leave it full of water on the draining board and put your plastic cartons and orange peel in the bin, not on the table. I'll collect the kids on the way back. I'm taking your car. My boot isn't big enough for your family groceries and there will be too many bums on seats."

She deposits the basket on the staging in front of his lotus shins and steps back As she turns to go her heel drills into the raked gravel and she strides away leaving him with neither peace nor appetite.

Richard Nakomoto unfolds his legs, rises to his feet and folds his arms. He turns his back on the basket and contemplates his display of bonsai: living beings, venerable, ancient and apparently immortal. Some indeed are over a hundred years old. They were brought from Japan to London by his great-grandfather, Yoshi Yuuki Nakomoto, and displayed at the exhibition of 1909. Richard lives to serve them.

Eventually a shimmering silence settles over the garden, followed by perceptions of birds squabbling on the roof of the shelter and wind in the cherry trees.

Ignoring the basket he walks from the bonsai sanctuary to the yard behind. Here with their clipped roots cramped into pots stand younger trees, rank upon rank, some hunted from the wild, others torn from the rich compost of dank and derelict gardens. Each specimen is chosen for its potential. Thereafter the genius of the gardener must get the most out of it. He pauses with satisfaction before his Juniper Chenensis in the Cascade Style, and then before the twin trunks of his Storm Damaged Scots Pine. He feels the approval of the ancestors over his shoulder.

He takes the knife from his pocket and moves along the staging cutting back a leaf here, a twig there, and pinching out errant buds. Even so, within the limits of their revered status and the discipline of their traditional calling, the diminutive trees still struggle to express their immortal souls.

On separate staging by the far wall stand the apprentice-pieces made by the next generation of the Nakomoto dynasty. Single cuttings of berberis and ivy claw for water over jagged rock, groups of hawthorn saplings matt their hair-roots in shallow trays. The youngest Nakomoto has grubbed up an errant cotoneaster seedling from the drive and wired it into the requisite twists and bends in a blue jar.

Richard moves to the brick path between the raised beds and pays his respects to a flowering crab apple and a dark pyracanthus. They are on furlough in the rich garden soil where a spell of undisciplined nature will thicken their woody trunks and make trees of them. In due course he will trim their roots, re-wire them into their final pots, and weight their frail branches with a skilled nicety that will make them weep without breaking. Even after the weights are gone they will stay true to form.

Three more days and his wife will be home with the new baby. He contemplates the event with pleasure. He much prefers his wife's cooking.

GAIL KELLY

Cherry

DAVID MCVEY

A Song Remembered

The metal Jacob's Ladder clanked and shuddered from the depths of the Subway station and deposited me, not in heaven, but on a windblown, sloping piazza that dipped towards a long canyon of pedestrianised street.

I turned and looked up the gentle stone-flagged slope. The canyon continued up the hill, bending to the left a few hundred yards ahead. Forbidding modern buildings glowered down at me. Surrounding me was a frenzied murmur of talking and shouting and laughing, broken by the desperate music of buskers and the whoopee whistles and barking, batterey-operated dogs sold by the hawkers.

Everywhere, everywhere people. The thought struck me that surely only on a medieval battlefield could people have congregated before in such numbers, in such proximity. Laughing, prosperous teenagers, perfectly turned out in fashion uniforms, milled about, exuding self-confidence, carrying string and cardboard bags bearing the names of expensive clothes shops. Other teenagers, in near-identical branded leisurewear roamed like packs of feral animals. Elderly tourist couples - German? American? - took pictures of the crowds, of the buildings, of each other.

This urban canyon was a whirling, bubbling cauldron of purposeful, determined, rather grim hedonism. Everyone except the hawkers, the *Big Issue* sellers and, perhaps, the worshippers filing out of a lunchtime service at the church down the hill, were there to consume as much and as conspicuously as possible.

But what about me? Why was I there? Why had I alighted from the Subway at this particular station, ascended Jacob's Ladder, and stood, almost afraid to move, among the throng?

What is the purpose of your visit? That's what they ask you in immigration, isn't it? Today I didn't know. I didn't remember why I'd even boarded the Subway - or where.

'*Big Issue*, sur? New yin jist oot the day.'

I smiled and shook my head. Graciously, I hoped.

'Nae bother, sur. Hiv a good yin.'

I had to make a decision. I couldn't stand at the Subway station entrance all day—or could I? No, I had to take responsibility, so I began to walk slowly, carefully up the hill towards the corner of the canyon. I slalomed between the strolling, standing, running, skateboarding crowds. The barrier of buildings in front of me was defended by a rampart of steps on which groups of laughing students sat, drinking from cans and bottles. High above them, a giant video screen flickered and beckoned like a false god, urging me, urging everyone, to buy things.

Then I noticed a statue, a gaunt thing, a tall green ghost wearing broken, twisted spectacles. I remembered that it represented someone who had been called 'Father of the Nation.' I couldn't recall why, nor did his name come to me. Some tourists were taking pictures of the statue. I don't think they knew who he was.

The canyon turned sharply to the left and then led, canal-straight, across a gleaming metal river of road, and began to rise again, gently, into the distance. The thin strip between the canyon walls was moving, rolling in waves and eddies and by-currents. People, so many people; each individual was, perhaps, purposeful and focused and intent on its business, but in the mass they were no more intelligent than an army of ants crawling over a rock. In fact, they *looked* like an army of ants. I shivered, and then continued up the canyon, pausing briefly only to ford the car-river.

I refused my ninth proffered *Big Issue* and wondered whether I ought to phone someone. All around me people barked, laughed, bellowed, swore or giggled into mobiles: why not me? Perhaps I could call someone who would be able to explain why I was here, why I had come into the city. Explain, even, who I was? But I could think of no-one to call, no-one to confide in. A quick check also confirmed that I did not have a mobile anywhere on me. Did I even own one? I couldn't remember.

I kept walking till the pedestrianised area ended and I found myself on a pavement beside a steady growl of traffic. I checked all my pockets again: a few coins and my Subway ticket, nothing else. How was I going to manage to get home? Assuming I remembered where I lived?

It seemed best, on the whole, to keep walking.

On my left the traffic moved slowly, sluggishly, like a lowland river picking its way among flat woods and fields: the pavement felt like a riverside towpath. At one point, road and pavement were carried on a bridge over a noisy, evil-smelling motorway, a ceaseless, frenetic cataract of vehicles. It felt strange to be standing looking down on such hurry, such perpetual movement. Immediately I felt uncomfortable.

I began walking again and, beyond the motorway, began following a quite different kind of street. I no longer felt like I was in a canyon but rising instead to some distant plateau of light and space. The buildings were sometimes high, but most were single storey (lower than the many double-decker buses that rumbled past) and in some places there were no buildings at all, just gap sites or car-parks that looked like lakes of many-coloured metal.

I passed lines of people standing beneath little structures with transparent, bulbous roofs. They wore serious, concentrated expressions as if they waited for instructions from God rather than buses. They seemed vacant and worried-looking and few of them looked at me as I went past, however closely I examined them. I wondered if their buses would ever come, and what would happen if they didn't.

I came to a crossroads where there was a small church building with a low, squat tower poking upwards and, further away, a football stadium with floodlight masts rising into the sky like dishes scanning the heavens. But everywhere else were buildings where people lived. Most windows now held not displays or products or advertisements, but curtains and ornaments and vases of flowers, sometimes even a gaunt head and shoulders interrogating the street outside. Once or twice I stopped to stare back. The occupants moved away after a time. So did I, once they had gone.

By now, as it grew dark, there were no crowds swarming over the pavements; just occasional pedestrians and the familiar expectant worshippers at the glass-domed bus stops. And, of course, just a few feet away was the angry roaring of buses and cars. And then it started to rain.

I stopped. The rain fell unseen from a hidden sky, sparkled briefly in the light bubbles around the street-lamps, and then cloaked itself again in its last microseconds before completing its mission of getting things wet. By now, I seemed to be the only person available to be wetted. Whatever I had prepared for as I set out from my forgotten home for whatever vanished purpose, it had not been rain. My thin, lightweight clothes were quickly soaked through. I had to take a decision, do something, go somewhere, be someone.

But I still didn't know who I was, nor even who I could *try* to be. The day, the shining city, the surging crowds, the whirring traffic, none of them had given me any clues to my past. What I now amounted to was what I remembered of today – and the clothes I stood up in. Should I try to retrace my steps and retrieve my life? Or ought I to try another direction?

I began, with a sense of the arbitrariness of it all, to walk purposefully along the pavement, beginning the process of fashioning a new person out of the sights, sounds, smells, memories and emotions of the day, the only day I remembered. It was oddly liberating. The rain eased and occasional passers-by were open-mouthed, taken aback to hear me belting out a song, cheerfully, lustily.

My first task, I decided, was to identify this song I was singing.

Tommy's New Friend

Tommy sat on the edge of an armchair and swung his legs back and forth. He was bored with looking at the old junk his grandmother was showing him. She had things that had come from somewhere in the attic, when Tommy's parents had been clearing it for extra space. After seeing her worn out toys and torn books that had been lost for years, grandma had got completely lost in her memories. Tommy tried to look interested, because most of the time grandma was nice, and Tommy knew she was often bored in her room, which she hardly ever left.

"Do you know who this is?" Grandma asked with a smile, showing Tommy a piece of paper that was yellowing at the edges.

The paper had a faded child's drawing of a smiling, purple little girl. Tommy tried to think who it could be, but the picture didn't really resemble anyone.

"Is it you?" he suggested.

"No, no. This is Lily, my imaginary friend. She was my best friend as a child. Purple was my favourite colour, so Lily always wore purple clothes. I used to tell her all my secrets."

Tommy looked at Lily. She seemed nice and friendly. Tommy had never had an imaginary friend.

"I want to have an imaginary friend, too. How do I get one?"

"Well, I don't know. I found Lily once, when I went to play by myself at the lake. She just appeared from somewhere. There aren't any lakes near here, but check the park or the woods, maybe you'll find someone there. I think I'll take a little nap now."

It had rained during the night and the grass still felt moist. Tommy jumped across a ditch, trying to avoid the water. He wanted to see if his imaginary friend would show up. He hoped to get one as friendly as Lily, but he wanted a boy.

At the playground Tommy finally found him, leaning on the swings and kicking sand. Carefully Tommy sneaked closer, as the friend didn't look as friendly as he'd hoped. But he could recognise him easily because, like Lily, he was dressed completely in purple. Although to tell the truth, Tommy would have preferred green.

The imaginary friend seemed really old, at least seventy. He had stubble on his chin, shabby clothes, and a beer belly. On top of all that, his nose was so long that it hung in front of the man's jaw. The nose was purple too.

"Hi. I'm Tommy. I'll be your new friend," Tommy introduced himself to the man with a welcoming smile.

The man glared at him and snorted. Tommy's smile became even broader and showed his teeth. The gesture of kindness didn't result in any kind of response.

"What's your name?" Tommy finally asked.

"Shouldn't you know?" the man snapped.

"Well, I don't. How could I know, we just met? Come on, tell me, please."

"Hmph. Fine, I guess Charles, or something. What difference does it make? No name is going to make me look any better."

"You are kind of fat," Tommy admitted.

The man's face turned bright red. He stared angrily at Tommy.

"My clothes are purple. What kind of colour is that?"

"I can't help it!" Tommy answered.

"Oh, really? And here I was thinking I was *your* imagination. Just my luck, to have my appearance dictated by some little dumbass. God, I hate kids."

Tommy started to get upset. This wasn't going at all like it was supposed to.

"Let's go play something," he said, and hoped Charles' mood would improve if they had a really good time.

"I guess so. You're the boss," Charles grumbled.

The pair headed towards the woods. Tommy kept glancing at Charles to see if he would express any interest in anything. But he just kept moping and looking disgustedly at all of Tommy's favourite places to play.

"I'd kill for a smoke," Charles mumbled just loud enough for Tommy to hear.

"You can't smoke. It smells terrible and it's bad for you," Tommy replied firmly.

"Hmph. All the same. It wouldn't be possible, anyway. I'd just burn my nose since it's right in front of my mouth. A person shouldn't have a nose this big," Charles muttered and glowered at Tommy.

Tommy pretended not to have noticed and finally they headed back to the playground. On the way Charles stuck his leg out and tripped Tommy straight into a puddle of water. Now he was all muddy. Even though Charles claimed it was an accident, Tommy didn't believe him. He'd noticed the man laughing to himself.

Tommy tried to play on the swings, but it wasn't much fun. Charles refused to join in or give him a push, and all the while Tommy was playing the man stared at him with open contempt. Soon Tommy got bored and decided to get back home. Charles followed him, dragging his feet and looking pleased with himself.

Tommy's mother was in the kitchen drinking coffee. Tommy sat opposite her looking miserable.

"Mom."

"What, Tommy?"

"I've got a new imaginary friend."

"That's nice."

"No, it's not. He's mean and ugly and he bullies me."

"Oh. Well. Oh dear," mom said, looking confused.

"What should I do? I have to play with him, since he is my friend."

"Umm, I don't really know. If he really is your imaginary friend, I guess you could make him do whatever you want. If he's mean to you, just make him pinch himself, or something."

Tommy smiled. Of course he could, Charles would have to obey him. Tommy turned around in his chair and grinned at the man standing behind him. Charles stared back viciously.

"If you do that, imaginary friend or not, I'll smack you one across the head. And hard, you stupid brat," he growled.

Tommy's face fell. He wasn't sure whether Charles could actually do it or whether it was just an empty threat, but he didn't want to take the risk. The man had really big hands.

Tommy got up from the chair and shuffled towards the living room. He heard a crash behind him and turned around. A large pile of clean plates, waiting to be put away, had fallen from the table. Charles was standing next to them, smiling smugly.

"Tommy! Watch where you're going. That was nearly all our plates," mom said angrily.

"It wasn't me!" Tommy shouted.

"Don't lie to me. They didn't fall by themselves. Now get out of the kitchen, so you won't step on the pieces. I'll clean this mess up. Like I don't have enough cleaning to do already."

Tommy spun around angrily. He couldn't believe how unfair mom could be sometimes. Then he heard another crash. A flowerpot had fallen off the shelf and there was dirt everywhere. Once again Charles was standing next to the mess.

"Tommy, I know you did that on purpose! There's no need to take it out on me if you're having a bad day. And don't think for a second you're allowed to go and see your friends after this. If you don't know how to behave, you can stay at home for a few days until you learn. Now get out of my way so I can get this cleaned. And you better not break anything else, or you're in a world of trouble, mister."

Tommy stared furiously at the brightly smiling Charles. And mom was stupid, too. Tommy had just told her about Charles, and still she blamed him. He couldn't help that he was the only one who could see his stupid friend.

Glumly Tommy walked to grandma's room. She was awake, although a little drowsy. Tommy sat in a big armchair by the bed. Grandma immediately noticed that something was wrong.

"What's the matter with our Tommy? Couldn't you find a friend for yourself?"

"I did, and he was stupid!"

Then Tommy told grandma the whole thing. Charles stood by the chair and seemed a bit embarrassed when Tommy revealed the way he'd behaved.

"Oh my goodness," grandma exclaimed when Tommy had finished. "Tell me, Tommy, is the man in the room right now?"

"Yeah, he's standing right there. You can't see him."

"Don't be so sure. After all, I do have some previous experience with imaginary people. Help me get started and tell me, what does this Charles look like?"

Tommy told grandma about Charles' beer belly and purple clothes and giant nose. Grandma stared at the spot where Tommy had told her Charles was standing, and little by little she began to focus her gaze on him.

"Alright, now I can see him. What an extraordinarily ugly man", she finally said to Tommy.

Charles blushed, but didn't seem angry. He fiddled with his collar.

"Why have you been bullying our Tommy? You should be ashamed of yourself, a grown man," grandma said in her firmest voice and stared at Charles sternly.

"I am terribly sorry, ma'am. Terribly, terribly sorry. I'm just a silly old man, I've never really learned how to get along with children. I wish I could take back the way I behaved. Tommy is obviously a very good boy, and he is very fortunate to have such a fine woman for a grandmother. My most humble apologies."

Having said that, Charles clicked his heels together and took a deep bow before grandma. After that he bowed to Tommy as well. Grandma looked satisfied and she smiled at Charles.

"Tommy, do you accept the apology?" she asked.

He nodded. Charles smiled, but didn't even glance at Tommy. He kept staring at grandma.

"If I may say so, madam has the most beautiful blue eyes," he said.

Grandma laughed. Little red roses appeared on her cheeks and she wiped a strand of hair from her face.

"Don't be silly. I'm an old woman."

"You're a woman in her prime. The years are kind to some people and they age like a fine wine."

Grandma laughed again. Tommy thought it sounded very beautiful, grandma seemed much younger than usual.

"Nonsense. Though I must say that I think I was wrong when I called you ugly. Your nose may be larger than average, but it merely adds personality to your face," grandma said to Charles, who was absolutely squirming with pleasure.

It seemed to Tommy that grandma was batting her eyelashes quite a bit. He also thought that she and Charles were acting funny. They kept grinning for no reason. Even though grandma seemed perkier than Tommy had seen her in a long time, she was ignoring him completely.

"I think I have to go now," he said and got up from the armchair.

Charles and grandma turned to look at him.

"If you won't mind, I think I'll leave Charles here. I don't really need an imaginary friend, I have enough things to do," Tommy continued quickly.

He left the room. As he was closing the door, he heard grandma laugh again at something Charles had said, then as he moved away he heard no sound from the room at all.

The Two Bogles

Bogles roam the hills looking for ways to cause mischief or harm to unsuspecting people lost in the hills at night.

AILSA BLACK

Louie the Sheepdog

*Louie is a sheepdog addicted
to lime lollipops.*

Photo Alan Cairns

Ailsa Black was born in Balleymoney and brought
up in Dumfries and Galloway. She spent four years
at Grays School of Art in Aberdeen where she
completed a BA[Hons] in Graphics and Illustration.
She has since combined working part time in the
voluntary sector, with freelance illustration work.
After college she moved to Edinburgh where she
spent the next ten years working in the voluntary
sector in community care and as a freelance arts
worker. In 2000 she moved back to Dumfries and
Galloway to work part time with people with
dementia and to continue her illustration work.
Throughout this time she has completed various
freelance commissions for illustrations and cartoons. Recent freelance
illustration clients include The Scottish Executive, Home Plus Scotland
magazine, Baby and You magazine and Dumfries and Galloway Health
Board.
She currently lives in Carsethorn, a small coastal town on the Solway Firth
with partner Alan Cairns, a freelance photographer.
To contact Ailsa Black, e-mail ailsa.black@btinternet.com or visit
www.ailsablack.com

AILSA BLACK

Every full moon the big cat steals another of his sheep and Louie just can't run fast enough to get it back. Then he overhears the cat talking to himself about his passion for porridge and how when eaten every day this unleashes his energy.

Louie ditches the lime lollipops and eats porridge daily until the next full moon. Powered by the porridge he out-runs the big cat and returns the sheep to safety.

AILSA BLACK

The Grumpy Gardener

The grumpy gardener is fed up having his vegetables eaten by the garden animals and decides to take things into his own hands.

So Deftly Himself

JB PICK

With contributions from

Tessa Ransford is past president and committee member of Scottish PEN. She is a poet, translator, editor and cultural activist. Tessa initiated the annual Callum Macdonald Memorial Award for publishers of pamphlet poetry in Scotland, www.scottish-pamphlet-poetry.com. She is at present Royal Literary Fund fellow at Queen Margaret University.

Diarmid Gunn, is the nephew of Neil Gunn (1891 -1973), the novelist, critic, and dramatist who emerged as one of the leading lights of the Scottish Renaissance of the 1920s and 1930s. Gunn was arguably the most influential Scottish fiction writer of the first half of the 20th century. JB Pick with FR Hart is Neil Gunn's biographer.

Stewart Conn is a recipient of Scottish Arts Council, Society of Authors and other awards. His most recent volume of poetry is Ghosts at Cockcrow (Bloodaxe 2005). He is also an editor of many anthologies, including *100 Favourite Scottish Poems* (Scottish Poetry Library/Luath Press, 2006).

Alastair Reid is a widely published and anthologised poet, translator, notably of Borges, and contributor to the New Yorker magazine. Born in Whithorn, Galloway, he currently lives in U.S.A. and has spent much time in the Spanish speaking world. His Collected Poems is due out in 2009.

Hazel B Cameron is the administrator of the Scottish Pamphlet Poetry website, editor of the Scottish PEN newsletter and recently became a full-time freelance writer and poet. Two of her pamphlets have been short listed for the Callum Macdonald Memorial Award.

Roderick Watson is professor at the University of Stirling where he is director of the Stirling Centre for Scottish Studies. He was General Editor of the Canongate Classics since the start of the series and is co-editor of *The Journal of Stevenson Studies*. His most recent collection of poems was *Into the Blue Wavelengths* (2005) published by Luath.

Alan Riach, poet and Professor of Scottish Literature at the University of Glasgow. He is the author of Representing Scotland in Literature, Popular Culture and Iconography (2005) and four books of poems, most recent Clearances (2001) published by Scottish Cultural Press.

Photograph opposite courtesy of Richard Macfarlane

JB Pick, So Deftly Himself

"When the establishment of the Callum Macdonald Memorial Award was announced I submitted a pamphlet just to show support for a really valuable venture, and was astonished when you rang to say I'd won." These are John Pick's words. The judges for that first award in 2001 were unanimous in choosing John's booklet, *Now*, from the thirty or so entries and it proved a best-seller at the pamphlet fairs.

Photograph by Mike Knowles

> Now is being out of time.
> What is measured is not now.

In this booklet as in each of the annual series of these gems, whose cover illustrations are by artist Gene Pick, there is a message from 'Dr Quantum', e.g., his presidential address, his paradox, his theorem, his physics, his metaphysics class. The series is collectable for these if for nothing else, but there is much else among these enigmatic and profound poems and aphorisms, including a sparkling humour: the three donkeys, for instance, in the poem 'The Philosophers' (in *Evening Light*) two of whom were clever and relied on 'Ontology' and 'Theology' whereas the third said 'Hay' and survived. In *Now*, we have 'Dr Quantum's Paradox':

> "In sticks and stones of here and now
> The hidden secret lies;
> All my solid theorems show
> That Nothing satisfies."

John Barclay Pick, who has recently turned eighty-six, is not only a wise and gifted poet, but also a perceptive literary critic, a talented biographer and novelist, whose historical novel, *The Last Valley* was made into film starring Michael Caine and Omar Sharif. Having chosen to join the Friends' Ambulance Unit in the war, rather than finish at university, John then volunteered to work in the coal mines. Later he worked in a family knitwear business, before being able to devote himself to writing. Erudite especially in the more metaphysical aspects of Scottish literature (Neil Gunn, David Lindsay, William Sharp) and having published in several genres, he became one of the editors of the Canongate Classics series, a publishing venture of the 1980s and 1990s.

Because of my own involvement, it is to John's contributions to *Lines Review* that I would like to draw attention. They go back to number 79 in 1981 where he is writing about G.S. Fraser, claiming that "To him poetry was not a mine to be exploited or a costume to be worn but a country to live in, to explore and to cultivate with loving care." And discussing Kenneth White in number 114 (1990) Pick finds there is too much jotting of fragmentary notes and suggests that "A poem… is the total absorption of significant experience and its re-creation as a formally vital whole." He suggests that the aim should be for the poem to be "so deftly itself that we won't notice the poet." That last comment and the one about 'a country to live in' could be aptly made in praising John Pick's own poems. In an essay in *Lines Review* number 116 (1991) entitled 'Form, Insight and Possibility', we probably have a neat summation of John's own credo for poetry. He concludes: "It may well be that the poems waiting to be written now require us to move away from the extreme tonal and metrical monotony of contemporary verse and to accept the wild variety of formal possibilities available, while retaining integrity of meaning and purpose."

It is hard to find better words to describe John Pick as a writer or as a person than his own. In his biography of Neil Gunn (with F. R. Hart), *A Highland Life*, Pick writes about Gunn's intuition of what he called 'delight' or heightened reality – a quick movement of inner flame – and also the 'inspiriting' atmosphere created by Gunn's presence. J.B. Pick has poems on each of the four elements in *Lines Review* number 118 where for 'Fire' he writes:

> God wrote no programme; there is only fire
> Which streams through substance as desire,
> Burning the heart of human-kind
> Into a passion of the mind.

And here is a conundrum:

> evening light by the river
> reading the code of a lost secret
> this   now   otherwise
> sun   moon   shadows.

It is a poem I have composed from some of the titles of John Pick's poetry pamphlets! The integrity of the man and of the writer makes him indeed 'inspiriting', someone I am grateful to know.

Visit Tessa Ransford's website www.wisdomfield.com

Things

Things cannot vanish, but they do.
Perhaps the impossible is true,
No key will fit the designated door,
And nothing can be certain any more?
When one day we turn and see
The long forgotten absentee
Lolling where an object cannot be
We insist bad memory's the clue -
Dodge, evade and won't admit it's true:
Things cannot vanish, but they do.

From Sun Moon Shadows 2006

The bat

A mouse in wash-leather
Bewilders the bright room,
Hangs for two breaths
Like a live Glove
From ridged white plaster,
Then with a sudden zig
Becomes imaginary
In soft night.

From water in a looking glass 1986

JB PICK

Night Drive

In silver silence as we drive
Each tree, each chimney takes its turn
To grow significant beside the moon.

By the Loch

My face in the water drifted off.
The trees, too, looked strangely
At their own absence.

In reverse

Look in the mirror: what do I see?
Myself the wrong way round.
Reverse the image: who is he?
A stranger never found.

From Perhaps 1998

Messages

Light always notices water;
By that transmitter
Winks its silver messages
Through inner space.

From water in a looking glass 1986

Messages

The Blackbird sings with liquid grace
"Nothing at all is out of place".
That parrot squawks in ruffled rage:
"What about me in a rattling cage?"
The coal black crow prosecutes the case:
"There's something wrong with the human race,
It's blind and cannot read the code
Or find the rock where the treasure is stowed."
The blackbird sings with liquid grace:
"This is the place! This is the place!"

From Otherwise 2004

Dr Quantum's Presidential address

"The obvious remains invisible,
Taking the form of holes round nothing:
Avail yourselves of the non-existent,
Grow in your garden acres of surprise."

From A Lost Secret 1995

The Adventures of Dr. Quantum

Dr Quantum went too far,
Inventing particles so abstract and bizarre
His Nobel Prize caused comment in the bar.

The lecture ends, and none too soon.
Dr Quantum draws a pale balloon
And blows it till it bursts: "Look, there's the moon!"

They lock poor Quantum in the loony bin.
He pricks on toilet paper with a pin:
"The universe is holes where light gets in."

The warden enters; Quantum isn't there.
A burning pencil dances in the air:
"Behold the absence which is everywhere."

The Black Hole

Through this black hole they rush,
The living and the dead
To form another universe
Upon a left-hand thread.

Well at the World's End

Here is the lost well; hidden by cobwebs,
Where the water boatmen row in secret.
The water's keener, fresher, stranger
Than any gush invented by a tap.
Why then do I only visit it
When the rusty tank goes dry?

From A Lost Secret 1995

The Wood

This is the hidden wood
Where all the lost birds sing.

From Sun Moon Shadow 2006

The Puzzle

This is the puzzle set by time:
Out of the dark unconscious slime
Crawled the sublime.

From By the River 2005

The Theatre

We don't mime
In the theatre of Time;
The wounds are real:
We are what we feel.

From Being Here 2001

On her birthday

If you're not here,
Here is nowhere.

From Evening Light 2007

Funeral

The temporary arrive
To bury the dead.
The ceremony is brisk.
By the gate, poppies,
Fragile and perky,
Celebrate their ignorance.

From Evening Light 2007

Morning

Light explains itself;
There's joy about.
Everything sings -
Even the choir of doubt.

From This 2003

Evening

Light and darkness marry,
Creating white flowers.

From Being Here 2001

Full Moon: 3 a.m.

To be here waking is to act the spy:
I beg night's pardon—and goodbye.

From Reading the Code 2002

Now

NOW is a word
That lies asleep.
It goes bad.
It won't keep.
But if it should wake,
Look out!
The moon will shine,
The trees sign
The dead leap
The heart shake.

This

A door has opened into This -
The wild exactness of what is.

From This 2003

The message

That is the message of the dead:
Take heart from absence.

From Well? 1988

The Obvious

The obvious is what I cherish:
Each day's wonder at what is.

From Evening Light 2007

Poem

If I call her and she sees the flower
There is no need to write this poem.

Poetry

Poetry is wise music –
Grief, wonder, time spent –
A form of physic
For which words are lent.

From Reading the Code 2002

JB PICK

The Real World

Once upon a time there was a boy named Thomas Dobham who was always known as Dob, which suited him because he couldn't learn things at school. The maths teacher used to stare at him in a strained and fishy way, and sometimes he would shout and throw chalk. His name was Potter, so he was known as Pot.

"Dobham," Potter said, "You are an idiot. A deliberate idiot."

Dob thought this an enchanting phrase and muttered it to himself between breathing until Potter threw chalk and shouted: "Dobham! What are you muttering?" and he replied "Deliberate idiot, sir."

Mr Potter gave him several hundred lines as a punishment for insolence. Dobham wrote the lines in very wobbly writing with blots. When Potter saw the lines he groaned in a peculiar way and put both hands on the top of his head as if to prevent his brains from flying out through the bald patch.

"Dobham," said Mr Potter, "what is your ambition?"

Dob thought for a bit and replied in a small voice, "To be real, sir."

"Real?" said Mr Potter. "What do you mean, real?"

Dob didn't know, and eventually Potter groaned again, more soulfully this time, and told him to get out.

On another occasion Mr Potter told Dob, "Your arithmetic is so bad that the problems you have attempted are farther from solution than the ones you haven't attempted at all. Tell me, what am I to do with you?"

Dob thought about this. "I might be able to do real sums," he suggested.

The class tittered and muttered. Mr Potter smiled thinly and held up a hand for silence. (The left one. His right hand was clutching a piece of chalk.)

"Real sums, Dobham? What are real sums?"

But Dob didn't know.

Mr Potter groaned. "Then perhaps you would consent to do these sums for me? And try to understand the simple principles on which they are based?"

Dob tried. He tried so hard that he was too busy concentrating on the explanation that he couldn't understand the simple principle on which the sums were based.

A girl called Heather passed him a note. It said in fat round writing, "What are real sums?"

Dob found he knew the answer very clearly. He wrote underneath in very wobbly writing with blots, "Real sums are sums where the answer matters." He wished he could always tell people things as clearly as that. Why couldn't he? Because you have to see something before you can say it.

Dob had found that it was no use appealing to his father for explanations that teachers had not the patience to give. His father was always annoyed when Dob expressed a doubt about the world. "You'll see what's real soon enough, my lad," he said, "when you've got great big hulking sons to feed and clothe and keep out of prison. That's what's real - working, eating, and sleeping, and don't you forget it."

Dob didn't forget it, but he couldn't help asking stupid questions such as, "Do you like your work, Dad?"

"Like it?" said his father, growing quite red in the face, "Why the devil should I like it? Anyone that likes his work is a bloody freak, if you ask me. It's bad enough having to do it without being expected to like it into the bleeding bargain."

Dob's mother told Dob's father to mind his language, and Dob's father said he did mind his language, he minded it very much indeed, it was just the sort of language his job deserved, and he would see that it got it. After that he went out to the pub.

Dob's father worked in an office at a factory that made shoes. Dob once asked whether his father wore the shoes that were made at the factory, and his father said, "Not bloody likely."

Dob decided that he didn't want to work in the office of a factory which made shoes.

The problem of where Dob would work sometimes made his father jerk about irritably. "The sooner he leaves school the better," Mr Dobham said to Mrs Dobham. "He doesn't learn anything. His reports are bloody... his reports are shocking. It's a waste of taxpayers' money to teach him. But who would employ him? He can't do anything."

"Nonsense!" said Mrs Dobham. She was an expert at saying 'Nonsense'. The way she said it would have made Genghis Khan blench. "Of course he can."

"What can he do, then?" asked Mr Dobham.

Mrs Dobham looked righteous, and her head wagged a bit but she didn't go so far as to reply.

Mr Dobham gave a spiteful nod and went to the pub.

It wasn't that he drank a lot or had a lot of friends at the pub, but the pub was the place to which he went. He went because he went. If he hadn't gone there he would have had to go somewhere else, and there wasn't anywhere else he could think of to go. When he was there he waited until it was time to go home. Then he went home.

It was what is known as 'a way of life.'

On Saturday he went to the football match if there was one, although he didn't much like football. He always had a down on the referee and several players on both sides, who he said were so bloody awful that they should be made to pay back their transfer fees in instalments. He said the ref should wear dark glasses and then he'd have an excuse for not seeing anything. Sometimes he took Dob to the football match, but Dob asked stupid questions such as, "Why don't they change patterns?"

"What do you mean change patterns? It isn't knitting."

But Dob didn't know.

As a matter of fact there was one thing Dob could do but his parents never heard about that.

He could fight.

He couldn't fight deliberately, but he could fight when roused. The other boys knew he was queer because the teachers thought he was queer, and tormented him by hiding his books, jabbering about him in groups, shouting at him, throwing things at him in class when the teacher wasn't looking, saying he had done things he hadn't, and stealing his food at lunch time. But when Dob got hold of one of the boys who was doing any of this he sometimes banged him until the boy fell down. As a rule the boy didn't like it and refrained from tormenting him for two or even three weeks. Once they set on him in a gang and Dob banged two of them about until they fell down. They all ran away, looking very pale, except the recumbent ones, who looked pale but didn't run away.

Dob was punished for hurting the recumbent ones and could offer no explanation of why he had done it.

It was shortly after this that Mr Potter said to one of his colleagues, "I'm worried about Dobham."

"Worried? You? I thought you had more sense. I thought you just taught the little perishers what they have no inclination to learn, not spent energy worrying about them. You've told me so, forty-three times."

Pot groaned. "Everybody's got to pretend something to keep alive, and I used to pretend I cared about the little perishers, but when I found out that it didn't do any good, I gave it up. But all the same, I'm worried about Dobham."

"What's he done this time?" said Mr Walnut.

"Well, he knocked young Lotus cold in the playground and then knocked Butter on top of him."

51

"Good," said Mr Walnut. "Well done, Dob."

"Yes, but that's the trouble. I had to punish Dobham. We're always having to punish Dobham. And yet there's no malice in him. He seems to take it all as a matter of course. He's not as stupid as he looks. In fact he may not be stupid at all. I tell you, Walnut, it's getting me down."

"Don't let it," said Mr Walnut. "I mean this very sincerely. Just concentrate on their maths and let their characters look after themselves."

"Anyone who concentrates on Dobham's maths will go up the wall," said Mr Potter glumly.

"It couldn't be worse than his French," said Mr Walnut.

Mr Walnut's remarks did not give Potter any comfort. One day he made Dobham stay behind and the rest of the class giggled and muttered, except Heather, because they thought he was going to catch it yet again and they were very pleased.

Mr Potter blinked at Dob, not knowing how to begin.

Dob stood looking thoughtful. "Mr Potter?" he said.

"Eh? Yes?"

"Do you like teaching?"

Potter looked sharply for signs of insolence on that amiable face and found none. He refrained with difficulty from groaning. "Why do you ask?"

"Well, my father doesn't like his work, and I've been thinking about that, and I just wondered."

"People don't expect to like their work," Mr Potter said. "They have to work to earn the money to live. It's a sum, Dobham - so much work, so much money."

"You mean, the harder people work the more they get paid?"

"Yes. Well, no, not exactly. Some people work very hard and get paid very little. It depends on the sort of job you have."

"What sort of jobs get paid best?"

"Oh, the heads of big companies, judges, financiers, Prime Ministers."

"Is that because their jobs are real jobs?"

"No," said Mr Potter definitely, and wondered why he had said that. "What do you mean, real?"

But Dob didn't know. Mr Potter realised that he must get himself and the interview under control. "What job do you want when you leave school, Dobham?"

"My father says I'll be lucky to get a job at all because I'm no good at anything."

"Well, that's what I wanted to talk to you about. Couldn't you make a real effort to get ahead with your work for this last year so that you will have a chance of passing your exam? Your future depends on it, you know."

Dob thought a bit. "It doesn't seem to have much to do with effort," he said.

Mr Potter wanted to shout "Nonsense, Dobham!" and throw chalk, but after all he was trying to understand the boy, so he must go through with it however bad for the nerves the experience might be.

"What has it got to do with, then?"

"I don't know, sir."

Mr Potter groaned inwardly but made no sound. He closed his eyes and waited, tapping his fingers on the arm of his chair.

"Sometimes," Dob said suddenly, "I just see something as if I was wide awake and I think, 'So that's what it's like!' and I look round and everyone else seems to be asleep. But if I tell someone what I've seen they don't know what I'm talking about."

Mr Potter didn't know what Dobham was talking about but all the same he felt a vague excitement to discover that the boy did have a brain after all.

"What sort of thing do you mean, Dobham?" Mr Potter said. He was disquieted to notice the tinge of sarcasm in his voice.

Dob noticed it too. "I don't know, sir," he said.

Mr Potter groaned. The urge to throw chalk grew powerfully within him. "I would really like to know," he said with heroic calm.

"It's difficult to explain." said Dob. "But one day I was looking at you, Mr Potter, and I saw that you could have been a real teacher."

Mr Potter felt as if fluid was being drained from the base of his spine.

"Is anything the matter?" Dob said.

Mr Potter found it impossible to reply.

"I'm very sorry, Mr Potter. I'll get you some water." Dob darted from the room and was back in a clatter bearing a cracked cup that had been used to hold glue and now held water.

Mr Potter took a sip. He looked round the room. It didn't seem the same. He had forgotten how appalling it was. He had forgotten everything. He looked at Dob's honest, earnest eyes and the sight made him groan.

DIARMID GUNN

I first met John Pick in 1973 at the funeral of my uncle, the novelist Neil M Gunn. The name was already familiar to me as it had come up so often in the conversations I had had with my uncle over the years. John was held in high esteem by him as both an intellectual companion and a true friend. The sad occasion that had brought John and me together was brightened for me by the feeling that I had inherited a friendship; our common interest in Gunn's work had ensured its blossoming. The sensitive and gently appealing biography of Gunn, of which John was the co-biographer, reveals a profound understanding of a writer who is widely regarded as being teasingly elusive. My uncle was indeed fortunate to have had as a friend a poet and writer to promote a better understanding of his work. It would be difficult to enumerate the number of occasions when I have had to advise people with a serious interest in Gunn to make contact with John.

John is a poet, writer and a critic of distinction. His erudition is masked by a relaxed and easy manner and his ability to make the most complex subject comprehensible. His interest in cricket and sport in general add yet another dimension to his conversational repertoire, from which a subtle sense of humour is rarely absent.

Every Christmas I await a so-called Christmas card from Hollins* with eager anticipation and a sense of delight—a word so meaningful to John. It is more than a card; it is a gift in the form of a collection of haiku-type poems. The beautiful cover designs by Gene Pick, John's most talented and charming wife, add something magical to this offering in "word". The gift epitomises the sense of wonder and delight that permeate John's work and life. I only wish I could see him more often.

* Hollins—The Picks' residence in Galloway, Scotland.

Neil Gunn and a Very Peculiar Trade

In 1945 I wrote an article about Neil Gunn in one of those literary journals which nobody has heard of, and which last only four issues, and sent it to him through his publishers. In January 1946 my wife and I left war-clobbered London for the Highlands, and in April of that year Neil Gunn knocked on the door of our wooden bungalow beside Loch Broom when I was lolling in the bath. Neil was the soul of courtesy when a damp tousled apparition presented itself.

I think he called a) because he was in the area that day, b) he was intrigued by the choice of novels mentioned in the article, not knowing they were the only ones I had read at the time, and c) because of the detailed attention given to The Green Isle of the Great Deep, published in 1944, which remained his favourite book for the rest of his life.

At that date Morning Tide (1931), and Highland River (1937), and The Silver Darlings (1941) had all been both a critical and a commercial success, and his publishers rejoiced. They wanted him to produce a series of similar novels so that they could rejoice some more.

The Green Isle gave them a bout of the shivers. Instead of a traditional novel set in the Highlands, it was at once an account of the adventures of a young boy and an old man in the Gaelic paradise, and a profound examination of its transformation to a totalitarian society based on analytic mind-manipulation and drugged food. Fresh fruit was forbidden. He wrote: 'Love is the creator and cruelty is that which destroys. In between is the no-man's land where men in their pride arrange clever things on the arid ground.' It was a warning. All over the world the powerful are still employing cruelty, and arranging would-be clever things on all the ground they can find.

The fact that The Green Island sold well reassured Faber. But they didn't know what was to come.

When he called on us Neil was fifty-four and I was twenty-four. He decided to further my non-career, which then consisted of one book, and set out with tact and subtle persistence to persuade me to apply skill and common-sense to a strong story based on what I knew and had experienced, and to cut out the fancy stuff.

His patience was uncanny, and he soberly informed me that impatience was my chief characteristic. He was right. It still is.

In 1950, he induced Faber and Faber to publish the first novel of mine which passed muster. This is where life's tendency to indulge in irony kicks in. At the same time as he was urging me along the path of common-sense he himself was doing exactly what his publishers didn't want him to do – writing odder and more challenging books which explored 'the other landscape' – this one seen by someone who is fully awake.

The first of these books was The Shadow (1948) which was events seen through the eyes of a sensitive girl brought to the edge of breakdown by men who approached life through cold analysis. It's never easy to write as if you were one of the other sex. Did he succeed? Some say 'yes', some say 'no', but the book is alive.

The Silver Bough (1948), The Well at the World's End (1951) and The Other Landscape (1954) followed, and Neil found himself having to write to the puzzled Geoffrey Faber about The Silver Bough: 'I don't want an incident or character to be ambiguous or difficult, not even mysterious. But actually the book is full of symbols and bits of myth. Accordingly, there is nothing that the reader cannot go on thinking or wondering about.'

Just so. The book arouses a sense of wonder at seeing a known landscape as if for the first time, describes darkness and finds light, creating a sense of warmth and humour. Marvellous.

Then suddenly, to surprise Faber again, Bloodhunt (1954) is a simple straightforward story which says exactly what it means without any need for bits of myth, legend or explanation. It's a pure masterpiece.

In 1956 he wrote his last book, The Atom of Delight, an evasive, meditative, philosophical avoidance of autobiography. It didn't sell. Yet it's a book which still attracts admirers all over the world, each of whom feels 'it was written for me.'

Neil himself said, 'When I finished The Atom of Delight I felt it was the end of my youth and now I'd really get down to it ... But the energy wasn't there.' He was sixty-five at the time and unwell. He lived to be eighty-one, and always set out on his daily walk along the shore with assumed vigour, breathing deeply and waving his stick to encourage himself. And me.

Some critics resent his later writing. They think he's insulting them by writing something they don't quite understand. Perhaps he's too simple for them.

The more you read Neal Gunn the more you appreciate his variety and depth. He's undoubtedly the greatest writer the Highlands has produced. It shouldn't be forgotten, either, that he spent the years between the ages of thirteen and fifteen with his sister in St. John's Town of Dalry.

Neil didn't like to be classified as a literary man. He said he wanted a relationship with nothing so much as with life itself. Well, he had plenty of experience in life, and if you contemplate his career you can't help coming to the conclusion that writing is a very peculiar trade.

STEWART CONN

It seems only fitting that this should appear in *Markings*, as the last time I conversed with JB Pick was on my way home the morning after I'd read at The Bakehouse, Markings' arts venue in south-west Scotland. He and Gene had kindly invited me to call for coffee and a chat – taking the alternative hill route an added attraction. It was the first time I'd visited Hollins. Indeed John and I have met on but a handful of occasions, and corresponded sporadically, down the years. This, though, does not reflect the extent to which – and areas in which – he has happily impinged on me.

For a start and though he won't know it, he is constantly within arm's reach. Swivelling my desk chair I can select one of a stack of booklets of poems he has sent over the years, as Christmas cards. Occasionally when things hang heavy, I take one out to enjoy its nuances and aperçus, to absorb his love of nature and lucid words of wisdom. They place a nimbus round time, the way Evening does in one "As gold light celebrates / A colloquy with shadows". Their intellectual clarity and spirituality, as free of pretensions as of religiosity, must surely be the essence of the man.

A little note with one explains our first contact: "It suddenly occurred to me to send you this... because there are so few of us left who knew NMG". It was through privileged entry into the orbit of Neil Gunn, back in the Sixties, that I became aware of JB Pick through Gunn's admiration and affection for him. Then came his own writings, and his editing with Ross Hart of *Neil M. Gunn: a Highland Life* and by himself, of Gunn's *Selected Letters*.

As a humane and enlightening critic and lover of literature – the two don't always go together – he seems to have stayed true to his lights, by word of mouth and on the page. In his own work or reviewing that of others, as in his forays into myth and legend, I get the feeling that as a standard-bearer for Gunn and for the Scottish literary tradition his stance and integrity are above fashion, his values hard-won and rock-solid. This certainly is the view of those who have respected his diligence on Canongate Classics and other projects.

Trying to start my car after that visit, it so happens, I found I'd left my lights on. The battery was flat. Luckily there were jump-leads to hand. At the risk of patness but given the occurrence, I'll end by suggesting that some people, never mind some writers, can be a drain on one's battery. Others are a selfless source of inspiration and energy. JB Pick is for so many people emphatically in the latter category. I warmly congratulate him on being a true member of the fellowship.

ALASTAIR REID

It was, I think, in 1947, while I was visiting Neil Gunn in Dingwall, that Neil took me to visit the Picks on the west coast. I was not long back from war service in the Navy, and although I had begun to write, I had met very few writers. What I remember from that meeting with John and Gene was the warm conversation, the ranging curiosity, the endless absorption in words, words, words. Soon after that, I left Scotland for the United States, and although John and I shared a deep immersion in Neil's writing, we met only briefly over the years.

It was when I began, a few years ago, to spend the spring of each year in Galloway, and discovered that John and Gene lived close enough for weekly meetings, that we have reconnected; and our conversations have become a large part of the pleasure of returning.

Not long ago, a Colombian poet whose work I have translated said in a letter "The best thing about literature is the friends it brings us." John's presence, his impish humour, his sparks of insight, his delight in language, leave me always with just that feeling. I treasure him as a friend.

HAZEL B CAMERON

JB Pick became a judge of the Callum Macdonald Memorial Award in 2002 when my first pamphlet was short-listed for the award. It was during that award ceremony that I first met Tessa Ransford and soon after she persuaded me to help John Cant with the new Scottish Pamphlet Poetry website. JB Pick was one of our first and most generous supporters despite not being on the internet and considering himself "...a contemporary of the dinosaurs." His beautiful little poetry books were an instant success and have continued to be each year since. His first entry form was neatly typed out on a typewriter with only minor splodges of tipex! He later moved on to a word processor though my most recent note from him was hand written as his "...word processor has retired hurt." I think it is wonderful that despite not having the internet himself, he has been willing to embrace it. He has certainly added to my enjoyment of administering the site and I have appreciated not only his joyful support but looked forward with pleasure to receiving his latest pamphlet each year.

Professor Roderick Watson

I first met John in —it must have been 1986—
when I was asked to join the team that was to
launch the Canongate reprint series of Scottish
classics. He was an old friend of Stephanie
Wolfe-Murray and involved with the project
from the very start. I was pleased to meet 'J.B.
Pick', a name I had come across on the only
study then available of David Lindsay the
radical, neglected, uneven and craggy genius
who wrote A Voyage to Arcturus. John remained an enthusiastic and
insightful critic of Lindsay's work and he introduced two of his novels for
the Canongate Classics series.

John is a generous reader of other people's work, a prolific reviewer
and a good critic in his own right. He edited the Gunn Selected Letters and
of course he wrote (with F. R, Hart) the definitive Neil M. Gunn: A
Highland Life (1981) followed by his own critical biography Neil M. Gunn
(2004). His study The Great Shadow House (1993) was a telling analysis of
what he sees as a special tradition of metaphysical fiction in Scottish
literature —an interest that goes back to his fascination with that most
unconventional of authors David Lindsay.

John is a novelist himself, of course, and a modest man. I remember
we were talking together about whether historical fiction ever manages to
convey a real sense of the 'pastness' of the past in books and films, and I
was raving about an excellent and unfairly forgotten film (something of a
cult film today, though) starring Michael Caine and Omar Sharif called The
Last Valley. When I had finished telling him how good I thought it was, he
remarked quietly that he had worked on the screenplay with the director
James Clavell, and that it was based on a novel he had written in 1959. The
next time we met he gave me a copy of the book. I still have it.

Working on the Canongate series with John, together with Tom
Crawford and Stephanie, and latterly with Jamie Byng, Cairns Craig and
Dorothy McMillan, we soon found that this was a man who had read
everything. For over 16 years, John's contribution to what was, I think, an
important and valuable project was immense. His delight in bringing what
he called 'hidden gems' back to light was infectious and inspired us all. He
had an acute ear for well-written prose (and an unforgiving one for leaden
lines) and he would often cite particular passages in his reports, or read one
aloud to make his point. It was such a pleasure to work with this gentle
man of letters.

In 2001 he won the Callum Macdonald Memorial Award for a small
volume of his own poetry, and in fact he has been producing these lucid and
Zen-like verses for many years in small volumes designed by his wife Gene.

There is a balance in these poems between the classical clarity of the epigram —rational and astute— and a saving sense of further mystery, of what cannot ever be wholly said. This speaks volumes about the acute and unpretentious nature of the man:

What is so
The behaviour of what is in fact the case
Avoids all theory with ambiguous grace.

PROFESSOR ALAN RIACH

From childhood's hour, I have carried with me the encounter with a long film called *The Last Valley*, and a reading of John Pick's novel on which it was based. In the film, at the end, the soldier-captain played by Michael Caine dies, and the wandering scholar Vogel, played by Omar Sharif, survives and takes the road again. In the book, both die at night, in the open air, side by side, but the vagabond scholar has the last word. He tells the captain that all his fighting and long wars were for nothing, but this, lying here under the stars alive, this is not for nothing. The final paragraph has stayed in my memory for nearly forty years: 'The villagers, armed and ready to defend their valley against all soldiers, were naturally delighted in the morning to find them dead. And yet the dead are not so easy to forget.'

J.B. Pick's novels – another fine book is *Out of the Pit*, about the life of miners – have perhaps been eclipsed by his work as the co-biographer of Neil Gunn and his involvement in the production of the Canongate Classics, making available essential texts of Scottish literature, but they are also a testament to the integrity, conviction and quality of the man and should be reappraised. In recent years, his little books of aphoristic poetry, *Being Here* and *Now*, have come as small surprises of delight. Complementing me kindly on my own book of poems, *Clearances*, John Pick made a remark that applies perfectly to his own work and the man himself: 'I particularly appreciated in the poems a sense of what is just out of sight.' His example of unobtrusive effectiveness is one of the things that make living in Scotland worthwhile.

BIBLIOGRAPHY

Expeditions. Fortune Press. 1944 (Poems)

Under the Crust. The Bodley Head. 1946 (Account of working in coal mines)

Out of the Pit. Faber and Faber. (Novel)

The Lonely Aren't Alone. Faber and Faber. 1952 (Novel)

Phoenix Dictionary of Games. Phoenix House. 1952; Aldine Paperback 1963

180 Games for One Player. Phoenix House. 1954

Spectator's Handbook. Phoenix House. 1956

A Land Fit for Eros. (with John Atkins) 1957 (Comic Novel)

The Last Valley. Little Brown. (U.S.A.) As The Fat Valley. Arco. (U.K.) 1959. (Historical Novel – filmed 1970 by James Clavell, with Michael Caine, Omar Sharif.)

The Strange Genius of David Lindsay (with Colin Wilson, E.H. Visaik) 1970 (Biography, criticism)

100 Games for One Player. Armada Books. 1974

100 More Games for One Player. Armada Books. 1976

Freedom Itself. Bay Tree. 1979 (Novel)

Neil M. Gunn: A Highland Life. (with F. R. Hart). John Murray. 1981; Polygon paperback. 1985 (Biography)

Selected Letters of Neil Gunn. (Ed) Polygon. 1987

Neil Gunn's Country (with others) Chambers. 1997

The Great Shadow House: The Metaphysical Tradition in Scottish Fiction. Polygon. 19993. (Criticism)

Cannongate Classics Anthology. Canongate. 1997

Neil M. Gunn: Writers and their Work series. Published for British Council by Northcote House. 1997

Poetry Pamphlets: Stones from the Beach. Bay Tree. 1979; Wind-Light. 1980; Games and Short Words. 1982; As Simple as Possible. 1984; Water in a Looking Glass. 1986; Well? 1988. A Lost Secret. 1995; Perhaps 1998; Now (Callum Macdonald Award) 2000; Being Here. 2001; Reading the Code. 2002; This. 2003; Otherwise. 2004; By the River. 2005; Sun, Moon, Shadows. 2006; Evening Light. 2007. All Drumlins Press

Biography Reviewer for the Scotsman 1981 – 2003
Member of selection board, Canongate 1987 - 2003
Reviewer for Markings since issue 23

Song for The Tinkler-Gypsies of Galloway

You touched the land lightly; so little was seen
Of your passing but tracks where a wagon had been,
And the ash of your fire whose blue-smoke haze
Made wisps on the sky on long summer days.

You touched the land lightly; you went as you came,
Each croft and each cottage continued the same,
No plough you had followed, no seed ever sown,
You moved on the earth – and you left it alone.

And one day they'd think of you, wondering when
They'd come on your camp-fire by Luce or Loch Ken,
But searching their minds and the years they would know
You had touched the land lightly, and left long ago.

based on the photographs and interviews of Andrew McCormick, C.1900

A Short History of Bamburgh

There are many histories: first,
The iron-red castle
Towering above the red-gold sand at sunset.

Next, the sea. How it roars
And quarrels with the islands: Longstone,
Its cold pulse of light.

Then bent grass and sand. Wind.
Squat willows, bones,
Skylarks singing over the whins to Spindlestone.

The Gamestone. The King's Baulk. The Worm Well –
Scraps and make-believe
Forged in the village smithy. What is forgotten

Between the Whistle Wood and the Blue Hemmel,
Matters most of all. Tomorrow
There are fields to sow. Deep in the Grove

Rooks, like old priests, squabble.

Katrina Porteous will be reading at The Bakehouse on September 27

Stinky

When you draw up here,
Down the hill to the rocket house,
The whitewashed Square

Brined in the past, that redolence
Of tarred rope, oak bark,
Rum casks,

And you lie awake
In the early dawn to catch the sun
Crawl up between

Billy, the coastguard watch-house,
And the castle;
While a robin

Scries from the pan-tiles
Of the hemmel,
And not one coble

Carves its wake
Through the flawless blue silk
Of the Haven,

You might be forgiven
For forgetting
This: the place

Was pigs, middens, yeddle,
Rotten kelp,
Fish livers reeking in the yetlin;

That the roof above your head
Is a tree, its roots
In herring guts.

'Stinky' was the local name for Low Newton-by-the-Sea.
The Square is now in the care of the National Trust.

On History

Thinking of how your father's father
could fashion a thistle
from a block of good Scotch pine,

I'm minded of Galatea's
tight little folded bud,
the tensile nub of the milk-white girl

and how I could never quite tell
who did what, and where,
and to whom-

whether it was he
that spoke through the chisel,
or the chisel that gave him tongue.

A Newgate Portrait

Oh yes, do paint my rosary
On this bare table:
It's papist I know,
But my only link to God.

And why do I have to look away from you?
You who are my guest
As I sit pensively serene
In my barred prison cell,
Convicted of murder
And sudden death my fate.

Yet suppose I did kill my mistress
and her two servants besides.
Well, it's bloody fame for me,
And a bob or two for you!

Still, my head is covered
In a clean white bonnet
And light, yes very shadowy
Shines on my face.

Sure, I am not praying
No, my arms are folded
Leaning on the table:
A dignified pose O Lord!

And do not forget
my pocket crucifix,
It is not a trinket!

You said yourself
I am 'capable
of any wickedness'

That's your verdict
About this woman's features,
Yet you refuse to face me.

But ask yourself
Is my dress really so sooty black?
Look how it billows!
I shall ascend into heaven
You'll see!

Note: William Hogarth's Portrait of Sarah Malcolm was painted in 1732-3 and is at the National Gallery of Scotland (catalogue no.: NG838) It is exhibited with the following information: 'Sarah Malcolm was executed at the age of 25 for the murder of her mistress Lydia Duncombe and two fellow servants in 1732-33. She is seen in Newgate prison where she sat for Hogarth two days before her execution on 7 March.'

Wild Strawberries

.

rough
against the tongue
before
the sharp burst
of sweetness
a strawberry
picked and placed
thoughtlessly
in my mouth
lifts me once again
up
on your tall shoulders
carried along
a Sunday morning
railway line
bending down
to pick wild strawberries
in the long grass

you showed me too
a lizard
and a grasshopper
patient
with my youthful slowness
my inability to see
their camouflaged shapes
laughing at my surprise
as the grasshopper
flisked
out of sight

remembering another time
other shapes
hard to see
against the shapeless
heat of foreign jungles

kneeling
side by side
lifting the berries
to our red mouths
somewhere
up the line
a whistle blows

.

Family History

We meet, shall we say,
on the grey, planned streets of Strichen,
walked past the net-curtained windows
along the regular blocks
of regular granite walls,
the neat little gardens
suddenly emptied by your footsteps.

Your waist went, quine,
your belly became whispers,
then a talking point, a village issue,
a parish disgrace.

The carter took you to Newburgh
at the mouth of the Ythan,
to a house that took you in
until your time came, till Isabella came.

There were questions, always questions,
but never answers, You never spoke
the father's name. That's fine by me,
let's leave it there. We can think
what we want, we'll never know
who lay with you there.

You're lying now, in the coldest bed
in Forveran, beside Bill Gordon, the one
who renamed you, the line
I never knew. Your daughter travelled
into my past, and is in me now
as surely as you are. I'll name you
without shame, Jessie Mutch,
great-grandmother.

Incident in a Small Community

That night there was snow-light bearing hard cold
to crisp cotton sheets, the crump of men's boots,
voices rasping against the bitter air the same name
over and over in bass, baritone but not belly deep
as the moan of the woman anticipating loss,
while the father waited, wordless, to comfort her:

that night, just beyond the edge of their farmlands,
taking direction from a spine of trees, they climbed
Stoneseat, Rushdown, came to Havenmoor
and a mound roughly covered, untouched by foxes,
the same length as the girl-woman who'd teased
each of them, thinking she knew the measure of each:

and because the men did, having fought together
at a time when life was cheap and skirt cheaper,
to this night each man avoids the others' eyes,
each remains apart scything his own narrow strip:
each prays that that night a stranger had passed.

Skin

the slow peeling of orange skin
unearths a dilapidated
misshapen yearning thing,
trying desperately to be an orange.

she fails at the first.

it reminds you of the eggs
you ordered from America
Louise for a girl,
Aaron for a boy,
named before the afternoon post
had even arrived.

it broke you, that orange.

cocooned from feeling,
feeding from your fears
and the world's swollen misery.

while inside, flesh
clung to an induced pip.

the fruit bowl mocks you.
another attempt,
you rouse from sleep,
the familiar expression;
cocked head
and soothing voice.

your husband jokes they
grow on trees, fetching
another from the larder,
failing to realize the attachment
you had placed on such
a small, unimpressionable thing
that had failed at the first.

an upside down frown
peeled from living skin.

Ripening

In green rodden time
I wanted to be you.
Scarted my knee
on reuch scabbit bark,
stappit my pockets
wi hard berries praying
you'd run oot o supplies
an need mine.

You made planes wi balsa
an gaudy coloured tissue,
wheeched a sharp propeller
makkin contact wi the wind,
file I held the hint o the twine.
Seely tae chitter, ice-tangled
file you ignored me.

Aenoo, rodden branches
hing hunnerwechted, dairk
ripened, riddy for pickin.
Saft crame flesh, nae use
for the games we played
lang syne.

And I'm ower thrang
tae help flee your plane.
Thrang rubbin bricht berries
atween my finger-eyns,
slowly staining my lips
tae silk in the munelicht,

waitin for you tae land.

Play It Again Sam

My mother - my 82-year-old mother - has informed me she has a boyfriend and is going on a date!

This is not something I expect to hear from my mother on a Friday.

Friday is pension day and I *expect* to hear exactly how long she waited in the queue at the Post Office, and in minute detail, who was before and who was after her in that queue. I *expect* to hear that poor Mr Arthurs, bless him, waited a full half hour and all he wanted was an airmail envelope to write to his daughter in America. This is the daughter who insists Mr Arthurs should be using e-mail and that was the reason she sent him money to buy a computer. But Mr Arthurs says it wasn't e-mail that had got him through the war, it was airmail. I *expect* to hear that poor Mrs Vardy can't get her feet into a decent pair of shoes because of her chilblains and that there is now only £45 between Mrs Stewart and her 'Stannah' Stair Lift. I *expect* to hear that Mrs Simpson from number eleven knows for a certain fact that *her* from number ten has been at it again with the co-op delivery man.

What I do NOT expect to hear is that my mother has a boyfriend!

Nevertheless, she continued to inform me, enthusiastically and with what I considered to be rather more than *undue* affection, that the *boy*friend is one Sam Pickles, who my mother says was her first love and who she had never quite forgotten.

And I'm left wondering, *where* exactly did my father feature in all of this?

My mother said she had not set eyes on Sam Pickles for more than sixty years. He had left prison and moved away and the last she had heard he was on the merchant ships. However, to her amazement and I might add, transparently undisguised joy, he had turned up at the Age Concern formation dancing a couple of weeks ago.

I said, "Prison, mam! Did you say prison?"

She said, a bit too dismissively I thought, "Oh Joanne, it was something or nothing. These days he would just have to clean graffiti off the walls of the underpass."

Her tone changed, she said affectionately, reminiscently, "he was just a naughty boy really."

Then she said, "Anyway, Joanne, I'd like you to meet Sam."

My life is going from bad to worse. It seems my mother could have been a gangster's moll in a previous life and I have been lulled into a false sense of security with treacle tarts and rhubarb crumbles. When I put this to her, she said, "Oh for goodness sake Joanne, lighten up. Sam is not a gangster and never has been, he's a sailor and anyway, it's better than going out with pond life."

Lighten up! Pond Life!

She said I sounded just like my grandmother, who wouldn't hear of my mother having anything more to do with Sam Pickles when he went to prison, said he was a bad lot. Then Gerald, my father came along. The model of respectability in his trilby and his made-to-measure suits and his Fair Isle cardigans in autumnal colours, with pockets for his carefully folded hankies which had to be embroidered with a G and his nail file and his Fisherman's Friends. Then she added, more, it seemed, as an afterthought and probably for my benefit, "God rest his soul."

"Anyway," she said. "I'm going on a date with Sam. He's coming for tea on Saturday and I'd like you to come too."

I asked my mother what they intended to do on this date, don masks and striped pyjamas and take a trip around Wormwood Scrubs for old time's sake perhaps?

She ignored me and said they were going ten pin bowling and I wasn't to worry about her bad back as Sam said there were contraptions which, after you pointed the bowl in the direction you wanted it go, did the hard work for you. Afterwards, Sam said they could either stay in the centre for a couple of beers and a game of Pool, or else go into town for a pizza.

And *what* might I ask, was wrong with a toddle round the park and tea and toasted teacake in the café?

That night I woke up in a cold sweat. I dreamt my mother was a patient of Harold Shipman!

I didn't tell Lucy and Josh their grandmother had a boyfriend. It was too bizarre. I needed to get used to the idea myself first. Just as well I was to meet him on Saturday as Josh would be going to the fun-fair with Jack and his parents and Lucy would be in Starbucks with Chloe, making eyes at the new waiter who had, and I quote, eyelashes to die for.

Well... Sam Pickles impressed me as not so much a sailor, more a pirate. Not so much Captain Birdseye, more Popeye. Not so much a gangster, more a Bookies' runner.

He was wearing a collarless shirt rolled up at the cuffs, a red bandanna knotted around his neck and combat pants with braces. The body parts which I could see, his hands, knuckles and lower arms were heavily tattooed. He wasn't tall. My father had been tall. Sam had a round face, a ruddy complexion which I put down to sea spray and piercing blue eyes which twinkled impishly for an old man, I thought. He had bushy white side-whiskers. His hair was thin and combed straight back and, it needed a double take, I spied a wispy little ponytail tied with a red stretchy band at the nape of his neck. I felt faint. He wasn't wearing an earring, although I checked for piercings and both his legs were intact, but otherwise a parrot on his shoulder wouldn't have looked too out of place.

He was definitely a bit rough around the edges. What on earth did my mother see in him? She had said men were in short supply at the formation dancing, but there was short supply and desperation.

My father, before his retirement, had been a department manager in a large department store and had been an excellent ballroom dancer and indeed his father, an articled clerk, before his early demise, had medals for it. No whiskers, no tattoos, and definitely NO ponytails there, thank you.

Sam took my hand into both of his and shook it vigorously. He said although I was pretty enough I was not a patch on my mother for looks. My mother, in little girl mode said, "Sam Pickles, what *are* you like?" Then she went into the kitchen to make tea and to put scones and currant buns onto plates with doilies, while I was left to entertain Sam.

I asked him if he had any family. He said he had never married, couldn't keep his land legs for long enough. Said he would still be on the ships if he hadn't gotten too old. He had been living in Portsmouth with his sister when he retired, but she had died and so he'd come back up North. He had a strange, sea-faring sort of accent. I asked him if he thought things had changed. He said changed! He would never have recognized the place. Motorways and shopping malls everywhere. He had gone in search of the motorbike shop, which used to be on the High Street, but found it was now a Kwik Fit garage. He said he quite fancied another motorbike, had one when he was young. He said my mother could ride pillion and they could 'burn' up the countryside. His eyes glazed over. My blood ran cold.

Between the arch of his legs, his lean mean pullin' machine vibrates expectantly, then splutters and dies. He strokes it, he coaxes it. He revs, it stutters. He revs again, it pulsates. He revs again and it throbs; ready for action. He punches the air triumphantly and yells 'Born to be Wild' at the top of his voice. His unzipped leather jacket shows the printing on his T-shirt, 'A Friend with Weed - is a Friend Indeed'.

My mother, with hair by Kawasaki, is waving to me with one hand while clinging onto his waist with the other. She has 'Bat Outa Hell' printed on the back of her leather jacket, the fringe of which flies back in the sudden gust of takeoff. She's calling, "we're hittin' the highway Joanne, then we're hittin' the sack. Don't wait up…"

I glanced at Sam. He still looked miles away and he had a smile tickling the corner of his lips. Was he reminiscing or was he planning?

I asked him if, apart from my mother, there was anyone else he recognised from the old days.

He looked startled for a second. Then, clearing his throat he said there were one or two familiar faces around but he had trouble putting a name to them. He said there was one bloke in particular who he'd seen at the formation dancing who he remembered from the dances at the Palaise before the war. "Thought he was Fred Astaire with knobs on, he did. Still does if you ask me, can't think of his name though."

Then he called to my mother in the kitchen. "Gwen, who's that bloke goes to the formation dancing; thinks he's the dog's bollocks?"

My mother called back and said she couldn't think who he meant.

Er, excuse me! *My mother*, trying to think of someone who thinks he's the dog's bollocks!!

"You know who I mean, Gwen. Done up like a ponce he is, smells like a whore's handbag. Looks like that poofter off the carry-on films. Whatsisname?"

"Sid James." My mother offered.

"Sid James isn't a poofter Gwen."

Sam looked at me. I shrugged, "Kenneth Williams?"

"Nah. Kenneth Williams is a poofter Joanne, no doubt about that, but that's not who I'm thinking of. I'm thinking of that slimy bugger, pencil moustache, says ding-dong when he sees a bird he fancies; lecherous git."

I didn't think poofters fancied birds, but I bowed to Sam's superior knowledge ... him being a sailor and all that.

Then Sam clicked his fingers. "Leslie Phillips! That's him."

"Leslie Phillips, Gwen." He called to my mother. "I knew it would come to me sooner or later."

My mother came in with the tea tray.

"Leslie Phillips, Sam? I don't recall anyone by that name goes to the formation dancing."

Two days later my mother rang to tell me it was all off between her and Sam Pickles.

She had asked him if her best friend Sadie could go with them on their date as she and Sadie went everywhere together.

Sam had said, "Hell's bells Gwen, I didn't have you down as a dyke".

Now ... either my mother has finished with Sam because she has decided life in the fast lane is more than she can handle. Or, she has taken exception to the implication that she's a lesbian.

I tend to think it's probably the latter.

This short story was submitted through the BDS Literature in Libraries scheme.

GAIL KELLY—PRINTMAKER

Autumn

Gail Kelly's work is inspired by the ancient folklore of Britain and Ireland, in particular the legends associated with our native trees and the countryside. She has produced a series of linocuts based on the landscape and prints these designs by hand on fine Irish linen using a Victorian cast iron press.

She uses a variety of printmaking techniques, including linocut, woodcut, lithography and etching.

Gail Kelly studied printmaking at the Ulster College of Art and Design and at Louisiana State University. She now lives and works in County Down in Northern Ireland.

Gail Kelly, 32 Ballyalgan Road, Raffrey, Crossgar, Co. Down, Northern Ireland BT30 9NQ tel & fax 028 4483 1199; email: gail@alganarts.com www.alganarts.com

JOHN MURRAY

Age Concern

She'd do him in. That would be best. She looked over the breakfast table at her husband and took in his dishevelled appearance. It seemed as if someone else had dressed him — and in a hurry: his shirt collar was caught inside his tie, which had not been tightened, his cardigan was bunched on one side, and the sleeves of the sweater underneath strayed out unevenly. With pity she observed the shake in his hands. He spooned up from his boiled egg and as he carried it to his lips his tremble sent it dripping onto his front. Her sympathy turned to irritation; how could she keep him in clean clothes, it was like having a baby in the house. Bad as it was now, worse was coming, she knew that, and that's why she would have to do him in. It was the kindest thing. For years people seemed not to change, but once ageing began it was downhill all the way.

The same with herself. Her reflection in the mirror horrified her — the wrinkles, the hanging flesh, the strange spots that appeared from nowhere, and that was just her face. The rest of her body didn't bear looking at, didn't bear thinking about. Sure, you could get tucks and lifts, but that was to disguise the problem, like some shady car-dealer tarting-up an old banger to fool the gullible. You couldn't fool yourself.

Man and wife they'd been for over forty years; they'd been good years for her, and she was sure he'd been as happy as herself. But what had they to look forward to — more of the same, every day like the one before it, and every day a small dwindling, like the tide easing out, like a candle guttering into darkness.

What was she staring at. Had he forgotten to put in his teeth. He tapped them with a knuckle. No; they were in. "I think I'll do a Tesco run," he said. "We hunter-gatherers have to be up and doing."

How often over the years had he said that? "Have you made out the list?" he asked her.

"It's on the fridge. I'll fetch it. You put on your coat."

The kitchen seemed surprisingly warm. He'd left the ring on again. When he took the porridge off the cooker, he'd forgotten to turn it off. If anything happened to her he'd never cope, he'd have to go into a home. She could picture him sitting in some dreary common-room gradually going as gaga as the rest. She knew she was doing the right thing.

When she came back with the list he was buttoning his overcoat. "Look at your hair," she scolded him, "you're like someone who's slept out all night."

She went to smooth it down, but he pulled away. "You'll be spitting on your hanky next and rubbing my face with it. My ma used to do that when I was a wee boy."

"Your poor mother had a lot to put up with a son like you."

His face sagged. "Indeed and she did."

She tugged his coat straight and himself out of his melancholy. "Away you go. You'll do rightly. Maybe your check-out ladies are into rough trade."

He pulled himself erect. "Sergeant McLeod on parade. Chest out. If you've no chests, lean forward. Right turn!" He spun round and the room tipped. He held onto a chair. He carried on, but it was a weak voice that declaimed: "Fix bayonets. Up and at 'em."

"It's downstairs you're going, son," countermanded his wife.

Going into Tesco he took out his list and went round the shelves. When he found an item he crossed it off, it was the only way he could be sure of completing the job. Olive oil. He stopped to look at the selection — Spanish, Italian, Greek, French — so much choice; then there was first-pressing, virgin, extra virgin. What could that mean? He remembered a song from the sergeants' mess. Had the officers sung a posher version?

"Four and twenty extra virgins from the town of Inverness When the ball was over there were four and twenty less."

And what was this? Extracted by mechanical means. Was that a plus? The image of Greek peasants treading the olives seemed more fun than some fearsome machine chewing them up and spewing out the oil. Ah well, everything changes.

"Excuse me."

He looked to his right. A small grey-haired woman pushing a trolley was eyeing him. "Could I trouble you to hand me down that jar of honey. I can't reach."

"No trouble at all." He handed it to her.

"You're very kind." She looked at the jar: "I wish they wouldn't put the lids on so tight. It's a bugger to get them off."

"Indeed," he agreed wholeheartedly. "A bugger is right."

"I lost my husband last year. He used to unscrew things for me."

A riposte struggled to get out, but he suppressed it. "I'm sorry to hear that."

"Ach, what can you do. You have to carry on."

He watched her head for the shelf of cat food. Where in her shapeless form was the young girl she once was; the dreams of romance, the fires of passion dwindled into buying tins for a mog.

"You have to carry on," she said. Why? Why did you have to carry on. The thought preoccupied him. His last call was to the tobacco kiosk. He stood in the queue and scanned the array of cigarettes and cigars. "Smoking kills" was the boast on all the packets. There was a come-on for you, and by the size of the queue it was working. It puzzled him that his wife, a sensible woman was still puffing Marlboros. Was she trying to do away with herself? Then it struck him. It was like that fellow who'd fallen off his horse in the Bible — or was it his camel? — and became a Christian. All his purchases had a sell-by-date on them, a "Best Before". What happened when they went beyond that? They were thrown out. No-one wanted smelly yoghurt or squishy fruit or vegetables turning liquid. Away with them. He was past his sell-by-date, so was his wife. But they didn't have to wait to be thrown out. They could do the job themselves, exit under their own steam, self-propelled; jump before they were pushed. "You can't sack me, I quit."

He'd made a decision. It felt good. "Do you know something," he said to the woman behind the counter, "You're a dealer in death. You're worse than that Pol Pot."

"Pol Pot? Is he the fellow that makes the noodles?"

He handed over his cheque card. She handed it back. "That's you're library card, pal."

He gleamed at her: "Maybe I'm after a true romance."

The banter cheered him; he could still raise a smile ... if nothing else. On the way home he pondered how to do the deed. To push someone under a bus would be a messy business — besides, if they had to wait for the number 2 to come down Dalkeith Road, they'd more likely die of hypothermia. He wouldn't tell his wife; it would only worry her, and she would want to talk about it. In battle there was no time for that, it was action stations. As the man of the house, he would take responsibility for both of them. And he knew what to do. Hadn't he been a sharp-shooter in the Korean War, all those years ago. "Dead-eye Donny" they'd called him in the regiment, and he'd been proud of the crossed rifles on his cuff. An image of a raucous night in Seoul with his platoon entered his mind, and the youthful energy and comradeship drenched him in anguish. He had to stop and look unseeing into a shop window. Old age was like being on a battlefield, a survivor among the dead and the dying. He wrenched himself back, an old man, a plastic bag carried in each hand, shuffling home; but his mind was racing. He still had his old sniper's rifle and a box of shells. The rifle was in the hut with his gardening tools. And the bullets? Where had he put the bullets....?

At home Molly had come to her conclusion. Poison was the thing. She would do a spicy curry. He was always complaining that her dishes weren't hot enough; this time she'd concoct a vindaloo that would take his breath away. As to what to put in it, that too was clear. She was a fan of mystery novels and many a victim perished from eating the wrong stuff. Fungi: that was the answer. If they found them at the postmortem they'd put cause of death down to an accident by people old and confused. And she knew where to find what she wanted.

Once a week she went to an afternoon sewing class in Bruntsfield, crossing the Meadows to get there. In a clump of trees near the croquet club, often there were fungi, and among them a pure white eruption known as "Destroying Angel". Just one was all she needed; one would destroy a regiment, never mind two old pensioners.

It would be better not to tell her husband, she decided. He would only argue. It was something she noticed in herself as well as in him. If one spouse suggested something, the other sought to amend it. She hadn't the energy for a needless debate; her plan was perfect, it would be best for both of them.

While her husband was shopping, she set out across the Meadows. A grey morning exposed a wide green space too early for the footballers who would noisily occupy it later. There were two or three people walking their dogs. As she approached the trees, a ball whizzed past her straight into the clump, with a terrier after it. She could hear it scuffling in the foliage. Her heart stopped, the little beast would damage the Destroyer. Now what was it doing? That would hardly improve the taste. She couldn't bear dogs: lolloping beasts with no reticence or modesty, like adolescent males. It came out with the ball in its jaws and ran agog with satisfaction towards its owner. The fungus was standing white and firm. Keeping her gloves on she tore it from the ground and put it in her plastic bag. She worried how it would taste — there was no way she could find out. Perhaps if she cut it up fine, marinated it in a curry sauce before adding it to the vindaloo ... She was pleased with this stratagem, she wasn't senile yet, she could still think a problem through. Several tins of curry sauce were in her cupboard; she preferred to create her own dishes, adding spices as they took her fancy, but she always laid in back-up in case she had to produce a meal quickly.

She set to. She would keep her gloves on; better safe than sorry, she didn't want anything to happen prematurely. She chopped up the fungus, dropped it into a blender, added two tins of Sharwoods sauce and whizzed it round. From habit she made to taste it, but drew back just in time. Then she set about preparing the vindaloo; she was heavy on the spices, spooning in the cumin, turmeric, coriander, cardamom. She added a little chilli for extra bite and put the pot to simmer on a low heat. The jugful of steeping fungus she would add later, when the flavours were established.

After lunch — neither of them ate much — it was time for her class, the last of the term. It was working out perfectly; the dress she was making was almost finished. She would bring it home that evening and after dinner she'd put it on her mannequin in the bedroom and make the final touches.

Before she left, her husband began the washing-up. He had to keep busy, if he sat down he knew he'd fall asleep and there was no telling when he'd wake. He had too much to do for that. Narcolepsy, they called it: attacks of irresistible drowsiness. He shook his head. What next! Now he was a narcoleper; sounded like a drug baron with bits falling off. Should he have a bell to warn people? It was too much. He looked round the kitchen. What was that jug? It had white bits floating on top. Disgusting. Molly often forgot to wash pans and pots; he was always coming across dishes with leftovers. Poor soul, she was as bad as himself. He emptied the jug, washed it and put it on the drying rack. Now he had to find his rifle. He knew exactly where it was. He went straight there. When he found it he breathed a sigh of relief. He had been sure it was there, but he couldn't be sure, even when he was sure. So far, so good. Now. The shells. He had a box of them, and the box was ... His mind went blank ... He could visualised the box, but where ... ? Bloody memory going. If your memory went, then who were you? He ran his hand along the rifle stock, brown and polished. He remembered well enough when he'd used it in anger; those desperate days along the Imjin river when they held the Chinese advance. He'd been a man then, not this shambling poltroon he'd become. He pulled back the bolt, and there in the gleaming magazine was a single bullet. He closed his eyes. Could he do it with one bullet? What if he missed? And himself? That had to be done immediately. That was the next problem. God Almighty! Life was nothing but problems; one damn thing after another.

He could feel tiredness coming over him, like a fog engulfing his senses. He wanted back to the house, his head was growing heavier, he had to sit down; the necessity became almost a panic until he reached his armchair and plumped down. He rested the intolerable weight of his head on the chair and found oblivion.

In Bruntsfield his wife's class was coming to an end. Carefully she put her needles and pins in their case, packed her threads and thimble and began to unbutton the dress on the dummy. It was finished. She wasn't sure about the buttons; she might change them when she got it home.

"That's a lovely dress, Molly," said one of her classmates. "You could go to a wedding in that."

"You'd need a hat to go with it, all flowers and fancy doo-dahs," said another.

"You'd need a man all flowers and fancy doo-dahs," said a third.

They'd been a jolly group, always up for a laugh.

"Let's go for a wee drink, it's our last class and we'll invite Mrs Finlay."

Molly hesitated. She remembered the vindaloo, and she remembered the sauce that was to be added to it. "I've things to do for the dinner."

"The dinner'll wait. You have that man of yours spoiled to death. Give him a ring, and he can do whatever's needed."

What a good idea. She would go out with the dressmakers for a last soirée, a sort of wake before the event, and Donald could add the sauce. That was only right. They had shared so many things, it would have been a shame to shut him out of the final act. She had her mobile with her.

The ringing of the phone woke him. He struggled out of the chair.

"You've not fallen asleep." It was an accusation.

"No. No. I was ... was reading."

"Oh, aye! Well, there's something you can do for me. I'm going for a wee drink with the girls. I won't be long, but it'd help the dinner if you'd add the sauce to the vindaloo and stir it in well. Can you do that?"

"Course I can," he waxed indignant to cover his confusion, "a man that held back the Chinese..."

"The vindaloo's Indian," she interrupted him. "Now, tell me what you have to do."

He ignored this. "Now, where is this jug?"

"You can't miss it, it's standing next the cooker."

"It's as good as done," he told her. "And I don't want any singing on the stairs when you're coming home, or it'll be jankers for you." He put down the 'phone. That told her. He had to sit down again. The phone call had jerked him out of his doze before he was ready. He felt cold and his joints were stiff, like they needed oiling. It was perverse. What you didn't want stiff, stiffened, and what you did want stiff ...

He gathered himself. That was another thing; even simple tasks required an act of will. Old age was not for weaklings.

In the kitchen his senses came back to him. The jug. Where was the jug? The only jug he could see was in the drying-rack. His mind creaked looking for an explanation. He'd washed the bloody thing up. How was he to know that slop was part of the dinner. Now what? His wife would murder him when she came home. Steady the Buffs. Tight spot. Sergeant McLeod. Black Watch. Imjin River. Mentioned in despatches. Tight spots before. Sauce missing in action, believed dead. No, not bloody missing, bloody wiped out. Need reinforcements. He opened the cupboard and reconnoitred the tins and packages. He spotted two tins of Sharwoods Tikka Massala sauce. "I need volunteers," he told them. "You and you." In moments he pressed them into service; caps off, into the jug, stirred them well, then poured them into the pot. He put on the lid. "Mission accomplished."

When his wife returned he was in a cheerful mood. She regarded him with suspicion. "Have you been drinking?"

He looked at the clock. "Someone who's been AWOL for two hours is in no position to question the Home Guard."

She took the rebuke. "You set the table for me, and I'll heat up the vindaloo." In minutes the steaming dish was on the table. "I see," she said, "that I've become left-handed."

Without replying he swapped round her knife and fork.

"Where did you go," he asked her "for your drink?"

"Bennets, it's the nearest."

"Were you thrown out for singing?"

"Now, is that likely? We were thrown out for fighting. The two Miss Thompsons came to blows over the barman."

She tasted the vindaloo. It was hot and spicy, no trace of anything strange. Her husband was tucking in with enthusiasm.

"Your best ever," he complimented her, "a vindaloo to die for."

"Will we listen to Desert Island Discs?" They taped it in the morning and listened to it at dinner. She would keep everything as normal.

"Who's on it?"

"It's Siobhan Redmond."

"Who?"

"Oh, don't pretend you don't know. She was on the television the other night in that comedy programme."

"What comedy programme?"

"The one about ... about ... smokers. And she was in that play about the schoolmistress and that long-faced actor you liked ... what do you call him?"

"What do you call him?"

"You know him well. You said he reminded you of Humphrey Bogart."

"Is he in the comedy programme?"

"No! No!" She shook her head. It was hopeless. "Shall we just listen to the programme."

After the meal they sat back replete. "Full marks to the commissariat. That was great. It's put life into me."

That was the last thing she intended.

"Have a wee rest," she advised him. "Those dress buttons don't please me. I'm going to change them."

Upstairs she pulled the dress over the dummy and began the alteration. She burped gently, it had been a substantial meal, but she felt all right, though she'd read that the fungus would act quickly. To carry on sewing seemed silly, but she liked the idea. Her husband was always talking

85

about men who died with their boots on; well, she would die with her thimble on, her needle in her hand.

Downstairs the man of the house waited only to hear the bedroom door close. He rose from his chair with purpose, no after-dinner nap tonight. It was like the time before a battle; one thing to attend to, everything else fell away. He went straight to the shed. He picked up the rifle. He checked the single bullet, and came out into his little garden. The drowsy scent of the night-stocks pricked his senses. The night sky was clear, the stars far off. He picked out the Evening Star and there was the Plough. Was he doing the right thing? Could they still not enjoy the days left to them? He dismissed his indecision. He'd thought it through. They'd had their fair share of living, maybe more than their fair share; they should go while the going was good, and they'd go together.

When? That was the next problem. He was not daunted by it; he'd got this far, he'd finish the job. Focus, he told himself, focus. He couldn't shoot her face-to-face, that would be too distressing for both of them. She mustn't know what hit her; then he'd do for himself. He leant against the shed and considered his best opportunity. Against the curtain on their bedroom window he saw the silhouette of his wife. His throat went dry, and his heart pounded. This was it. He had the weapon ... he could see the target; it was exactly what he wanted. But what if he missed? He looked down on his hands holding the rifle; they were shaking. He couldn't do it. God help him, he couldn't do it. Sweat formed on his forehead and turned icy-cold. Some other part of his mind took over and he went back into the hut and trundled out a wheelbarrow and haughled down beside it. The grass was cold and wet, God Almighty, he'd catch his death. He slid back the rifle's bolt and made sure the bullet was in the breech, then pushed the bolt forward, closing it. He propped himself on his elbows and laid the rifle across the rim of the barrow. He squinted down the sight and fitted the cross- hairs exactly on the head of his wife. The years dropped from him and he became the young Highlander whose training had discovered a deadly marksman. Like a jungle predator his whole being was intent on the kill. He tightened his hold, his finger encircled the trigger. He squeezed it. The recoil wrenched a shout from him and sent him sprawling. He scrabbled to his feet holding his shoulder and looked up at the bedroom window. The curtain was blank. Blackness broke over him, the blood drained from his face. He held on the shed door until his head cleared, then stumbled toward the house. He was gasping for breath as he climbed the stairs, pulling on the banisters to get him up. He pushed open the bedroom door. There, face down on the carpet lay his wife, stiff and still, not a tremor, not a murmur from her, the dummy overturned beside her. His whole body winced at the sight, and blackness again threatened to overwhelm him. He leant against the wall and breathed deeply. His one thought was to finish what he'd begun. Carefully, holding on the banisters he stepped downstairs, straight into the kitchen, turned the switch on the cooker and opened the oven door. Awkwardly he hunkered down, the adrenalin that had sustained him flooding away, and he was an old, feeble pensioner. It reassured him as he put his head in the oven that he'd done the right thing. His breathing made a hissing noise, or was that the gas? Anyway, it was over now. He felt dreadfully tired, darkness was again coming over him and this time he welcomed it.

"Donald! Donald! Come on!" He was being shaken, then someone was pulling at him, pulling him out of the oven. His head banged painfully against the side, and he collapsed onto the floor, then struggled up to a sitting position. His wife rubbed a hand across his brow.

"Am I not dead?" he asked her.

His expression of bewilderment made her smile. "No," she said, "you're not dead, but you're a bit charred; were you pretending to be a baked potato?"

"I don't understand," he said, looking round him. He hadn't been the most attentive scholar at the Sunday School but he remembered nothing about coming back in your own kitchen. She sat down beside him. "And there's something I don't understand, though I have the notion that you might be the man to clear it up. Here I am stitching the dress on my mannequin when there's a crack through the window and the dummy's on the floor; one dead dummy. I must have fainted with the shock, but when I come round and stagger downstairs I find my husband with his head in the oven. Now what's that all about? I take it you were the trigger-man. Why did you want to assassinate my dummy?"

"I thought it was you."

"You thought it was me."

He reached for her hand. "We're past our sell-by-date, Molly. I thought it best we'd go out together."

She squeezed his hand. "You know, Donald, that same thought crossed my mind." She debated whether to tell him about the fungus. What had happened to that? She felt as right as rain, and he looked fine, apart from a bit of charring. She just might keep it to herself. It would be the poor sort of woman who didn't have a few secrets from her husband, and on her deathbed she'd have something to whisper.

"But why am I not dead?" He still looked puzzled.

"If you're trying to gas yourself, an electric oven's not a good choice."

"Electric! I thought we had gas."

"We did have gas — in our old house. We've only been here two years. Keep up, son; you'll miss your own funeral."

"I think I've just done that."

87

They sat quietly together, holding hands; such small intimacies were now to her as thrilling as in youth had been the scuffles of passion.

"We could go on holiday," she suggested. "Break the routine."

He nodded. It was a good idea.

"Why don't we go back to where we had our honeymoon."

An even better idea.

"Stride along the Via Tribunali."

Memory stirred in him. "Sipping grappa in the Piazza Bellini."

"And the pizzas," she recalled. "Real pizzas — Margaritas and caizones and and ..." She stopped; better not mention fungi.

He nodded, remembering. "We could go to that trattoria that did Viagra toppings."

They were holding hands again when the aeroplane circled, preparing to land. "Look down," she said. "Look, you can see Naples."

"See Naples." He repeated. Wasn't that a saying? See Naples ... How did it go? For the life of him he couldn't finish it.

DEREK HARRIS

Stolen

Thieves made off with a police Alsatian
Last night in the thickest fog.
Police are saying that have a lead
But, unfortunately, no dog.

Attracting Flies

Luke Abel walked stiffly from behind the screen. Doctor Frawlly, looking uncomfortable, watched as he buttoned his shirt. As he caught Luke's gaze, he pretended to write something on a scrap of paper; at times like this he wished he was a plumber.

"You better sit down Mr Abel, I have some very bad news, I'm afraid."

Luke crossed the room and sat down, with difficulty, opposite Doctor Frawlly. He tried to smile but succeeded only in producing a sickly leer. The doctor hummed and hawed for a bit, scribbling doodles on a prescription pad, mentioned all sorts of medical jargon.

"For God's sake doctor…"

The doctor composed himself. "Well you see, Mr Abel, I'm afraid… you're… dead." He felt so much better now that he'd got it over with.

Luke was struck dumb. For several seconds he stared blankly at the doctor.

"What?" he said, "Dead?" The man's bloody barmy he thought.

"I'm afraid so – as the proverbial doornail – although a coffin nail might be a more apt metaphor – I'm no pathologist but, at a rough estimate, I'd say, for about thirty six hours."

"You can't be serious? Funny sort of a joke if you ask me."

"It's no joke, Mr Abel. I've done the tests. Blood pressure zero, heart rate zero, brain scan negative. Rigor-mortis, early stages of decomposition. Oh you're dead all right. After almost thirty years in the profession you get to recognise the symptoms."

"But how can I be dead!" squawked Luke Abel. "I'm walking, talking, breathing, thinking…"

"Walking and talking you may be, but you are most certainly not breathing, always an essential prerequisite for being alive in my experience, and as for thinking, well according to the results of your brain scan…"

"Bugger the brain scan! If I'm dead then how can we be having this conversation. How many conversations did you have with a dead man?"

"Many, many," said Doctor Frawlly reflectively, "all of them one sided of course. Until now."

"And doesn't that strike you as odd?"

"It is unusual, but we know so little of life, even less of death. Death, you could say, is one of life's great mysteries." Philosophy was not one of Doctor Frawlly's strong points. "But surely you must have noticed the little things," he continued, "loss of appetite for instance, constipation, a general lack of motivation, stiffness; not to mention an extremely unpleasant body odour..."

"This is ridiculous," said Luke Abel, "I'm just a bit under the weather, that's all."

"We must face facts Mr Abel – and remember there are arrangements to be made, next of kin to be informed, insurance, funeral arrangements, a post-mortem..."

Luke Abel nearly fell off his chair, "Post-mortem!" It was less an exclamation, more a squeak.

"Standard procedure in these cases – sudden death you know – I could not, in all conscience, sign a death certificate without first ascertaining the cause, highly unethical. You may have been murdered for all I know."

"I demand a second opinion!" screamed Luke Abel.

The post-mortem, while being extremely unpleasant, was, surprisingly painless. It turned out the cause of death was some obscure congenital defect.

"You must've passed peacefully away in your sleep," the chief pathologist told him.

"That's a comfort," said Luke.

"Well at least you left us well provided for," said Mabel, his wife, "now about the funeral..."

"What funeral?" asked Luke.

"Your funeral of course. Who else do you know who has died?"

"No-one's burying me."

"Well cremation's out of the question. The family plot's already been paid for, and it's in such a beautiful location, you said so yourself."

"I am being neither buried nor cremated," said Luke Abel forcefully.

"Well we're running out of options," said Mabel, "and you have to consider the insurance."

"Stuff the insurance!"

"Self! Self! Self! That's all you ever think about. You know for a fact there can't be any pay out until after the funeral."

"But..."

"And then there's the neighbours. What happens when bits of you start dropping off all over the place. I would never live it down, we'd be social outcasts..." She started to cry. That was the *coup de grace*. What could Luke Abel do?

He had to stay in the back garden during the wake because of the smell. All the family attended, right down to great aunts and third cousins, old friends and work colleagues. Everyone said how well he looked – considering. To save on the expense of a hearse, Mabel drove to the cemetery in his (or rather hers now) Ford Escort with the coffin secured to the roof rack. Of course, Luke had to make his own way there, again because of the smell, and they wouldn't allow him to use the public transport because of environmental health concerns so he had to walk and, as a result, was late for his own funeral.

"There's not much room," said Luke, as he settled into the coffin.

"For God's sake, now he's complaining about the accommodation," said Mabel, "Why must you always find fault?"

"I was only saying."

The lid was screwed down and Luke Abel was finally laid to rest. And there he remains to this day. It's a nice spot. Up on a hill, overlooking the river. Very quiet. Not that Luke can appreciate any of this, buried, as he is, in the cold, cold ground, in the dark and damp, with what's left of him slowly crumbling away and only the worms and maggots for company.

But if you listen, if you listen very carefully you might hear Luke Abel calling out. He always says the same thing.

"I don't care what anybody says. I'm not fucking dead!"

This short story was submitted through the BDS Literature in Libraries scheme.

THANK YOU ELSPETH
retiring editor of Markings

ELSPETH BROWN

The Silent Smile

Carlos took some time answering the door. He felt his dog move to his side but she did not bark. "Lie down, Zoe," he said firmly. Careful not to knock over the dregs of his breakfast cup of aromatic black coffee, his fingers brushed round the refectory table he used as a desk and he strode confidently in a straight line for the door. The richness of the carpet brushed his feet until he felt it thin slightly where it had worn near the vestibule. He was annoyed with himself as he had to fumble for the handle. He liked to get it first time. His hand was on the bevelled edge of the centre panel. His fingers slid left to the cold metal handle.

The doorbell rang again. "I'm coming," He could not keep the irritable tone out of his voice. It made him feel slow and clumsy when people rang the bell again before he got there. He was too young to be slow and clumsy.

Now he was in the porch. The tiles felt hard against his feet and the air was colder. He had the brass doorknob first go.

"I'm Margot, from the agency," she said. A confident voice, a young woman's voice, but it was easy to be mistaken. He heard her step in without being asked and stepped back too far himself. His extending cane, which he always placed in the left hand corner, rolled on its tip and crashed somewhere behind him. Damn it!

Through the open door, he could smell trees drying after rain. The warning chip chip chip of a blackbird reached him. He stood still for a moment distracted by a fragment of visual memory drifting like a wisp of mist through his mind. He was six again; in his garden at home, and a blackbird, close enough for his fading vision to see shouted a warning. A ginger cat, glowing in the sun, stalked across the wet grass. It had been spring then too, when his lifetime's darkness enfolded him.

"I'm from the Agency," she said again.

"I'm Carlos. Come through." He had forgotten the cane and tripped as he stepped out of the porch. He felt like kicking it.

"Shall I pick it up?" She was beside him.

"If you like." Carlos was relieved she had come. He had some last minute changes to make to the lecture he was giving that afternoon. Not being fully prepared was stressful. He walked firmly ahead across the carpet, hands skimming the table until he reached his swivel chair and sat down.

His clock on the shelf intoned, "Eleven a.m." A masculine voice. He felt her startle. Probably wasn't used to talking clocks. "Sit down. At the table beside me would be best for the moment. This is where I work when I'm not on the computer." He smelt her perfume, he recognised it, couldn't name it just then but recognised it. He heard her pull out a chair.

"I'm Margot Reilly, the agency said you were a writer."

"But you haven't read anything of mine? Never heard of me?" He smiled to show he was joking. No response, only silence except the sound of nylon on nylon as she crossed her legs. "Well are you speaking to me or are you just going to sit there?" Her silence irritated him. It cut him out.

Margot Riley's brilliant smile faded, the smile that always got her what she wanted. Got her loved, forgiven, taken notice of, first by Daddy, then the boys at school. And now at work or play men usually took to her. She didn't have to try too hard. Well it wasn't just the smile but also because she was beautiful. She had been told so often enough. She was usually sent out temping for men because they were always pleased with her work and wanted her to come back. Not politically correct but practical. Though she knew she was an indifferent secretary, she had just drifted into it. She had wanted to go to university but had not been encouraged.

So it startled her a little, Carlos' absolute indifference - no worse, his irritation. She hadn't realised he couldn't see at all. His eyes were clear and looking approximately towards her.

"What do you want me to do?" She tried the little girl voice, automatically pouting, leaning towards him, her elbows on the mahogany table.

"Christ," exploded Carlos, "Didn't they tell you anything at the agency? I wanted someone mature. I need help to finish writing my lecture. I'm not happy with it and I have to deliver it this afternoon at the National Library. My secretary let me down at the last minute."

Margot felt strangely inadequate. He didn't like her, he was disappointed in her. And he was an attractive no frills red blooded male.

She felt like saying it wasn't surprising his secretary let him down, as he was an irascible bastard. But she didn't. She could see he was anxious about this talk and annoyed that he needed help. Instead she said, "Look, they didn't tell me much, but I'm here now. I'm no Einstein but I'm no dumb blond either." Where had that come from? Was it true people didn't take her seriously because of the way she looked?

"Do you want me to take notes?" She impressed herself with her brisk tone.

She seemed to have got it right for he smiled and said, "Okay, I'll explain how we can work together. I'll make some coffee. Come through to the kitchen with me." His smile was uncertain; difficult to smile without visual connection, she understood. He had run his hands through his dark hair and it was sticking up, making him look younger.

He walked through to the kitchen, his hands feeling confidently forward and he reached for the kettle with barely a hesitation. He felt for the switch. "Coffee all right?" He asked. "I'm afraid it's instant. Not as good but easier when you're busy." Margot nodded and smiled before she remembered and said, "Fine thanks." He filled up the mugs, one finger discreetly in the top of the cup to know when it was full enough. "Help yourself to milk and sugar. Take a biscuit from the tin." He hesitated, "Would you mind carrying the coffee through?"

"Of course not." Was it really so hard for him not to do everything himself?

She nearly tripped over the dog on the way back. "I didn't see your dog," she said breaking off a piece of her chocolate biscuit. He must have heard her or guessed what she would do.

"Don't give her anything to eat," he warned. "She's not allowed." The dog stood up and looked at her with hopeful brown eyes. Margot was tempted just to give the biscuit to the dog anyway but felt to do so would be cheating Carlos.

"She's a guide dog, and they could be distracted by titbits if they were used to getting them," he explained sitting at the head of the table. "Poor starving Zoe, come here." She hurried over to him, her feathered tail beating against the table leg. "She likes being a working dog, she's half collie and half retriever," he said stroking Zoe's head. "Of course she's not on duty just now, she knows she's working when she has her harness on."

"She's beautiful, what a lovely golden colour." That was probably a stupid thing to say, she could feel her face redden. What an effort it was when you couldn't just flutter your eyelashes. When you had to be real. And he's treating me like I was serious. What odd thoughts were coming into her head this morning. Why should she not be taken seriously? Was that her own fault? Did people who could see her treat her as if – as if what? Men – even Jamie, didn't take her seriously; especially Jamie. Jamie treated her as if she were delicate, as if thinking too much would tire her. Surely that was old fashioned. She loved his old fashioned charm, didn't she, didn't she? She looked up at Carlos. He was fondling the dog's ears.

"Is he more gold than brown?" He enquired. "Most people say he's brown."

"Well," she hesitated.

"Go on. I like to know about colours. I try to remember them. I could see until I was seven. Sight finally went at seven." He was matter of fact.

"There's a gloss on his coat, like pale winter sunlight, like the glow from translucent amber. A warm colour." She wanted so much to let him imagine it. It touched her to see how much he loved Zoe. It occurred to her that she would like to have a dog. Jamie didn't like dogs.

"The glow from translucent amber," he repeated.

"She's a beautiful dog."

"Right lets get started," He was suddenly brisk. "It would be best if you sat at the computer and I read to you what I want changed. Its been typed up already. I'll have to tell you where the changes are. He had a neat red machine in front of him. "This is my Perkins. Writes in Braille." He rattled in a few lines. "This is my Braille copy. I need to take a printed copy as well to give to the organiser."

She sat at the computer and was alarmed to see nothing on the screen. Of course he wouldn't see the screen. Perhaps the screen didn't work. He came behind her and said, "I'll put it on edit. My secretary left it on the right document."

Margot jumped as a solemn voice intoned, "Per-haps be-cause Hardy was a nov-elist, comma, as well as a po-et, he was in-ter-ested in the quirks..." The voice was solemn and morose

"Jesus, what's that?"

"That? That's Hal. Voice to help with editing. How else would I do it? The bit I want to change is further on. I've something about Hardy's interest in oddities of human nature, I want to put something warmer than oddities."

"Oddities is a bit circus freaky." She felt ill at ease in front of this blank screen. She had no idea what he wanted her to do.

"Scan on then," he said impatiently, "We certainly don't want freaky."

She tried switching on the screen. Nothing.

"I don't know how –" He reached over her impatiently, felt for the keys and Hal droned dryly on. "Para-graph in-dent ..."

Margot felt tears pricking her eyes. She had never felt so lost in a job. "I don't know why you called for me," she said quietly, "You seem to be able to do the work better than I can."

"Surely you can find the words quicker on the screen?" He sounded puzzled.

"The screen isn't on." She tried to keep the tears out of her voice. "I thought maybe it didn't work, you didn't ever use it..." She shrugged helplessly and didn't know how to show her confusion any other way that he would understand.

She expected an irritated put down. His hand gripped her shoulder. She could feel him shaking, with suppressed anger, she was sure. But he was laughing, trying to stop himself, but laughing. "I'm so sorry, Margot lass, I assumed you could see the screen. To think you were just listening to Hal droning on, and I'm asking you to pick out a duff phrase!"

"It's okay," said Margot.

"It's not okay. I upset you, didn't I? Forgive me. Just switch on the screen at the plug."

She was almost crying, then she was laughing. His hand still on her shoulder, they were laughing together as Hal intoned "Wom-en in Hardy's novels were bold comma sassy comma in charge comma and erudite full stop paragraph He was inter-ested in the cer-ebic and sensual oddities of human nature "Oddities! Got it!" They both shouted together.

"That's a bit over the top?" He tilted his head to one side.

"A touch arty farty?"

He laughed, "That's it, arty farty. Rewrite that bit for me? I bet you're a reader."

"How can you tell?"

"It's the smell, odour de library. I have a very developed sense of smell."

"What!"

He was laughing again. "Joke, joke. You said a few things, intelligent things, descriptive things. I don't have a sixth sense; I just use the ones I have flat out. And by the way I can smell your perfume, its Picasso."

"It is. Funny really to name a perfume after a man who sometimes painted women in bits." She reached down to pat Zoe who had moved to her side.

"So I've heard. I don't fancy a woman in bits."

They were both silent. The silence made him uneasy. There was something about this woman. The intelligence she didn't believe she had, how easily she had been upset by his annoyance, embarrassed because she thought it was tactless talking about the dogs colour. And how she had made him, if not see it, know about it. It was just so hard not to be able to do everything. He should be over minding by now. After thirty-three years in the dark. The feel of her shoulder under his hand; when he realised she was crying. Her honesty. Arty farty! .

"Will you help me make this talk less arty farty?" he asked. "Will you come with me when I go to the lecture theatre and make sure I am facing the audience?"

"Of course I will," she said. He could hear the smile in her voice.

97

Touching the Edge
for my friend, Alma

I am not from the blind world,
not yet, for dark can fall by chance.
You say you have friends
from both worlds,
blind and sighted. Are we then worlds apart?
Words link us, we talk for hours,
you aware when I am distracted
by a silent bird, the shape of a tree.
I return to orbit your unbroken
focus. You write as if you see,
though you have not seen for fifty years;
your final infant view a cat in an ochre aura;
a dying sun's last rays as you stumbled
terrified into a black hole,
between two worlds.
You learned to feel your way by landmarks,
bumps at road crossings are your moonlight
in the dark world.
Your stick rolls confidently from side to side
touching the edge of things, balanced
in both worlds.
Though aware of your loss,
you appreciate by touch and sound,
brain honed nuances and tone.
You write poems, read, listen, sing;
feel fluff in the sink turn into a spider,
make friends blind and sighted,
as you roll your white stick round the earth's edges.

Feeling the Day on Portobello Beach
for my friend, Alma

Warm oak front door, slippy, hard tile steps,
iron gate, needs painting, She dusts off the crumble,
steps onto the prom. Salt sultry air wafts from the shore,
the gentle swish of waves tells her the tide is high.
She walks towards the beach, ears strained for flying bikes,
children splashing in puddles, her shorts and tee shirt
so cool on her body, a summers day.
Gingerly she negotiates the steps, takes off her soft suede sandals,
toes wrap round the cool loose sand. Children laugh
but distantly. She knows she is facing the sea, a soft breeze
wafts a seaweed top note on air, clear from the river mouth.
She follows the hollow wind and knows she has stepped
from the building shadow. The glow on her skin
is the noonday sun. Entranced she steps towards the water
till she feels the chill lap at her toes. A dog paddles by,
close enough for her to feel the swish of his hairy tail
on her bare legs. She strokes his furry ruff, his upwards ears
tip tilted. Children call, Jarvis, here Jarvis!
She steps on cautiously, testing for the squish of jelly fish,
sharp shell, shelving shore, joyous with the sun on her back,
wind ruffling her warm hair, seabirds cries sharp in her ears
and around her the pulsing life of the shore and the sea.

Broth and Vitamin C

Ego and id, animus and anima, subconscious mind leave me alone.
I'm in charge and I'm fine, you hear me? Fine.
Construct no more protective obsessions
Blocking my thoughts with manic activity
stop interfering. I have only to think logically
And I'm me as I always was - before.
As for the dreams, the symbolism is so bloody crude
I'm ashamed that any subconscious of mine
should have come up with that crap.
Now I've burnt a pan communing with you.
In the midst of stress and death here am I
scrubbing a pan with a brillo pad, a practical Capricorn.
Subconscious take note. I'm in charge.

Not for me a Wagnerian welt angst, pale black weeded nobility
suffering with dignity. No, rather my nose is running,
I have the trots, drink too much and tell my friends
about my sex life in detail I could never achieve in Art.
So I muster another meal and try to keep those I still have, alive
with broth and vitamin C. I know I am whistling in the dark.
But only subconsciously.

Boat O' Rhone

Straddled across the Ken unkept since the last train
Beechum axed, departed from Mossdale to Parton
from Parton to Mossdale, you stand firmly enough
around scooped sleepers and couped waterlogged timbers.
Swallows swoop and feed signalling from your spars,
departure then arrival, leaving and returning, to find you
wood crumbling, stone sand flaking, iron rust redder
and fewer rash drivers daring to cross
where the Paddy line once rode.
Some wauchle across, skirting the pools
kicking skelfs through fissures to the limpid loch.
Before I feared to drive across it
though I studied it from water to russet arch
I could never dare to line up
with the solid planks. Feared to veer
to the rotten dropping timber, off the curve
to the left into the breathing woods
out of sight beyond the lattice loops,
cats cradle suspended between here and there,
the chasm between Mossdale and Parton,
Parton and Mossdale.

Between the leaving and coming of the birds
while the ferns grew darker,
the sandstone bled to the river flow.
A brush with the darkness befell me,
a tilt of the earth, a shift of alignment
a seismic tremor in the mind; a new proportion.
So I lined my wheels to the sleepers,
opened my eyes to the living woods
and drove to the far side.

This is viaduct on the old railway line from Stranraer to Dumfries which crosses
the river Ken. It was known as the Paddy line.

ELSPETH BROWN

The Hot Blooded One

"Anthony Hearn here." I am having real trouble speaking into my mobile. "I'll be back in the office in an hour." I shiver despite the April sun for there is a cold wind blowing from the Forth. I zip up my jacket.

An alcoholic drink is tempting but the aroma from an open door draws me into the warmth of The Coffee Mill. I need some space before I go back to the office. I suppose I could do something healthy like go to the gym, but like I said, I am cold and also a bit down, down in the mouth, ha bloody ha. Thirty-nine, well four days off forty, and already I have false teeth. Let's not get carried away here, a false tooth. Only last week I had to get my first pair of reading glasses. I feel round the inside of my mouth with my tongue. The roof is swathed in plastic like a cloche. I taste blood and wonder how I can eat. Are there really people going around with all this stuff in their mouths? Surely that plastic will dig into my flesh once the injection wears off. There seem to be bits of barbed wire clipped to two of my teeth. My nose feels frozen and could be running with snot for all the sensation in it. I hastily grab the piece of kitchen roll I use as a hanky and dab. It feels as if I have half a nose. How embarrassing that the young woman dentist should have seen me like this. It would have been easier as a man to man thing. If I increase my mortgage and get an implant, I hope it is done by a man.

The coffee is rich and warming, so the alive part of my mouth tells me. I wonder whose idea it was to give a Scottish flour mill an Italian ambience. A group at the next table is very interested in the history of the place. Apparently it had been a flour mill long before the city had engulfed it like a feeding amoeba. The original hewn stone walls have been decorated with false beams, too straight and without knots. These do not deceive the group at the next table. I get the idea they belong to some sort of history club. Idly I imagine what I will do when I retire.

The ceiling is low which accounts for the high decibels. The noise is like the buzz of bees in lime trees. It is counter pointed by blasts of sheep bleating laughter.

At this time of the morning the place is filling up rapidly, mainly with older people. I notice most of them are wearing glasses; some put them on to read the menu. I feel my new reading glasses against my thigh. I try to read the menu and all but the headings blur. Beverages. Not very Italian that. Bevies... I wish I had looked for a drink. Bloody teeth, why couldn't they grow in again?

The visit to the optician last week had been even more depressing. You only need reading glasses, for Gods sake, I tell myself. It was the way the optician had said it. She didn't look a day over twenty-four. Just natural ageing of the eyes, she said. Ageing! I don't think I've slowed up much. I could still play a passable game of squash. Maybe it's time to start going to the gym. Maybe not.

Menu. I hold it at arms length. I guess that is ciabatta by the length of the word and the shape. I'm hungry but don't know if I can eat anything. The girl serving me returns, obviously irritated that if I wanted something to eat I hadn't ordered it with the coffee. I can't face bringing out the reading glasses. The idea is still unfamiliar.

"Ciabatta, what with?" Perhaps she despises me because I am slavering blood. Surreptitiously I wipe my mouth with my piece of already bloody kitchen roll. I peer at the menu, fumbling in my trouser pocket for the glasses. When I look up again I see this woman stepping in to the cafe.

Poised by the entrance, she looks around. She will have to sit at my table; there aren't any others with free seats. The waitress is waiting for me to speak. I have gone off the idea of food but I haven't the nerve to say so.

"Ciabbatti with cheese." I sound drunk, the words slur. Is this my voice from now on?

"What kinna cheese?"

"Any old cheese." It comes out like a snake hissing. The girl shrugs and leaves.

The woman at the entrance has style, how do I deduce that? The relaxed poise as she looks round for a seat, the cut of her sleek dark hair, the fit of her jeans, hugging her racehorse bottom, and the sweater, a Mediterranean blue, the sort you can't get with cheap dyes. Since when did I become a style guru? I like the look of her that's all. She is on her way. "Do you mind if I sit here?"

I am suddenly shy, afraid to speak, afraid to open my mouth. What if there is blood on my teeth and I looked like Pterosaur, the sad one who died trying to get a mate in the T.V series, *Dinosaurs*? I have a brief vision of him forced to the edge of the group and howling to the sky for a female, fish blood still crusted on his teeth from his last meal. The females circle and choose the young dynamic, sharp toothed mates. He dies still calling. God I feel tears prickling. How helpless I had felt with that nubile dentist crunching and grinding with pliers inside my stretched mouth.

Surely I have been looking at this woman for an age with my mouth clamped shut. I nod to her to take a seat, trying to smile with my mouth closed. It occurs to me there is no reason why she shouldn't be a dentist or an optician. I try to see her in a white coat. It would suit her. She looks at me steadily as she pushes her dark hair back from her eyes. Her eyes are as blue as her sweater. I am smitten; it's more than sex, it's holistic. I want to dance, sing, turn cartwheels.

"Pension day." She remarks, reading the menu.

"What?" is all I can say. It comes out like a splat of sound as my tongue slides over the smothering plate.

"Pension day." She leans towards me confidentially. "Doesn't matter where you go, it's always like this on Thursdays. Cheerful lot mostly. Thought it might be quieter in here though."

I nod wisely afraid to speak again. I run my tongue round my teeth to clear them of blood.

"Can I get you a coffee?" I ask trying desperately to catch the eye of my surly waitress.

The words sound clearer, maybe I was not going to be struck dumb after all.

She catches the eye of the unsmiling one, who instantly smiles at her. "Just a latte thank you."

"Coming up right away."

"Do you know anything about Borges or Neruda?" She asks as if she were asking the way to the supermarket. And why should she not ask about Borges and Neruda rather than the supermarket?

"Borges and Neruda?" The hiss is back in my voice. I try again. "Borges and Neruda." Better. "Poets? Writers?" I say uncertainly and my brain is on search www.Borges.com

Labyrinths, reality, comes on screen, Neruda, cult film about Neruda, Neruda Neruda, there are ten entries none of them coming through clearly. "They are South American writers," I find myself articulating carefully.

"Yes, yes, this is excellent. Would it be a bore to you to talk about them? I have to talk about them and most people know nothing about them. Sad friends I have." She laughs.

"Why do you have to talk about them?"

"I'm doing this Open University thing, South American writers it's called, like you said. These two just get to me, especially Borges. He changes the way you see the world. I have this tutorial. I'm on my way there. And that's how I remember things. Talk about them. Thank you," she says as her Café Latte is served with a smile. My Ciabatta is plonked down in front of me. I can't even think how to bite it, especially while talking about Neruda and Borges.

"Tell me about Borges." I say, waving my ciabatta in front of my mouth and curling my lips round the edge. It feels as if only part of it is in my mouth, though an odd tingling has started in the absent sector. I

104

remove the food and put it back, intact but soggy edged, on my plate. "He wrote something about a tiger didn't he? A tiger of words and a real jungle, bloody mouthed, sabre toothed tiger."

Where have I dredged that up from? Search engines are raking through the debris of my brain. Student days of course. The last time I had interesting thoughts. Stella Martinez, she had read that poem to me. Stella and I had been together for five years. Was that when I had last been happy? I slurp some coffee trying not to let it run out of the frozen patch on my lips.

"Oh this is excellent. I'm not interrupting your peaceful coffee am I?"

I swallow some salty blood and shake my head. "Tell me what you think about Borges, or his work or whatever it is you need for this tutorial."

I watch her as she talks, distracted by the fluid movements of her hands, her enthusiasm. "I love that bit about, *'the hot blooded one, flesh and bone tiger.'*" She uses her arms in the continental way. She pauses for breath and drinks her coffee. "You really don't mind me disturbing you? I'm not usually so pushy. But to have sat down at the same table as someone who knows about these writers …"

"I don't really know about them." Why was I being so honest and not chatting her up and flannelling on South American writers? I have to admit that's what I would normally do with a girl I fancied. I have another go at the ciabatta and manage to bite off a bit on the left of my mouth. Chewing it seems impossible as my mouth is now beginning to hurt and my frozen nose has begun to tingle. I try to suck the bread and a chunk breaks off, rendering me speechless again.

"I'm Henrietta," she says "But everyone calls me Henny."

"Tony," I manage. I think of all sorts of clever things to say but can't say them. Did she expect me to call her Henny? Hinny? that was better. Some sort of high bred horse. No, wasn't it a sort of mule? I swallow the softened bread, just managing not to gag on it.

"I've never been here before." She says. "Was it really an old mill or is that pseudo?"

"No it was, Henny," I say. "If you look out of the window you can see one of the grinding stones on the grass at the other side of the millstream. If you look straight across the garden through the trees you can see Berwick Law on the estuary. Some of the people here look old enough to have come here when it was working." Wow, I can speak after all. I start to smile forgetting the bloody teeth.

"There's something about it on the back of the menu," she says, picking it up and reading it. I notice her small hands and slim fingers.

"Isn't that an amazing view in the middle of Edinburgh?" I ask, surprised by her lack of interest in the view.

"I can't see Berwick Law," she says, looking up from reading whatever it was on the back of the menu. "I've left my glasses at the optician to have the legs adjusted. I'm short sighted. Can't even see the wheel properly." She shrugs a Gallic shrug.

"I've had a tooth out." I say taking the glasses out of my trouser pocket so that I can read about the mill.

"I thought so," she looks at me closely. "There's a smear of blood at the corner of your mouth."

She folds her napkin and firmly wipes it away.

GAIL KELLY

Oak

ELSPETH BROWN

Reunion in Saffron Walden

As we look for things to recall
in the faces of each other,
a carillon of bells
wakes the swallows' young.
In the streets of the town
our memories are often skewed.
In overhung beamed houses
droppings drape the patched pargeting.
Cromwell stayed here, surely too plain
for the Tudor Sun Inn,
upper story dangling above the street.
On market days French sausages
and English apples gleam glossy on stalls
between hanging Indian cotton
and patchwork country throws.
Layered with other pasts
we reappear in our old college,
substantial ghosts. This
a reunion of friendships formed
when first away from home.
There is one from the other side of the world
who rejoices in a robin rare to her now. He lights up
a changeless summer garden, sunlit reunion,
highlights the variegated leaves, hare's tail grass,
red hot poker and phlox, roses in bud and blooms
wide to the sun, vulnerable to a changing wind.

Green Man in Spring

He rises clarted with dark earth of the old cold year,
hawthorns part for the green man in the wood,
green flush on ancient oak unfurls for him
as he is reborn primitive and lewd,
writhing to disgorge foliage
from his roaring mouth.
Roused from his dreams of playful days,
his sensual months of carnal sighs,
driven unseen by rising sap, raw rebirth,
solitary renewal in a hidden glade
until he mellows to rearrange the leaves
rakishly round his emboldened head.
Deep in the myths of old he lives
a callow puck again he thrives.

GAIL KELLY

Spring Garden

ELSPETH BROWN

The Johnstone Crocodile, Queensland

The Crocodile in the Daintree river
where rain forest meets the reef
curls in a cosy snooze like a newt in an aquarium
as the boat stealthily slides close to the mangrove trees.
Their roots breath air above the sluggish salted mud.
A tree snake dangles like a tangled vine sliding
cautiously out of sight of the gliding boat, though all eyes
are on the slumbering ten foot Johnstone Croc,
lazy in the damp heat, surely sated by some feast
we can only imagine. His lower teeth bristle outside
his pointed snout. I could stroke his rough hide.
His eyes snap open. Hard grey eyes, he is no newt
or gentle tree frog. His old cold stare is psychopathic.
"Never smile at a crocodile, never smile at a crocodile."
He prefers small mammals but big hairless ones will do.
But the banks and river rustle and ripple with easy prey.
He stares past me, waves his tail in irritation,
only momentarily disturbed. His eyes snap shut.

Infernal Nightmare

Reel round under the ground down through the funnel
swirl and twirl hear hells death knell, fall to abyss.
Staggering haggard fear the dread dark tunnel,
laggard hanging back for the last lustful kiss.
Lower layer in a heated cooling tower
lusty lovers, linger lost guilty glutted.
Cleopatra's asp clasps her in a last gasp hiss.
Helen in Hell, Francesca with her lover
in lascivious lust locked love, visited
by dreaming Dante. Virgil leading lower.

Hell hole

This would be one kind of hell.
To be entombed with golfers
trying to understand more than the nineteenth hole.
An underworld too organized
for dogs or dirt, bonfires and fog.
Rather give me the gloomy Styx and Charon's howl.
Only uplifting Third Reich art
with poems that never have any lines longer than any other
                                              lines in the stanza
and square gardens mown each week;
tulips in rows of matching colours.
No cats to dig them up,
no bats in lofts, no mice in wainscots.
My hell would be a jail of perfect people,
faces like film stars, bodies of top models
the set of Dallas; clothing colour coded,
all the horses Arab browns.
No piebald, skewbald, no gypsies, no ancient knotted veins,
fruit like waxed copies, irradiated.
The death of weeds.
Always imbibing just enough,
swimming only in sterile water.
No trying crazy things, knowing the limits.
Eternally doomed to being sensible.

REVIEWS

Clairvoyance: Selected Poems 1990 – 2007 by James Graham Pub: Matador ISBN 978-1906221-089 review by J. B. Pick

Words are natural and immediate for James Graham. He uses them to say what he sees without flourishes. His poems have plain strength and a salty flavour.

He strays into romance when his detestation of commercial society inspires him to make a hero of Jack Sheppard, the 18th Century thief whose uncanny knack for escaping from prison gave pleasure to the poor of his day, and Mary Bryant, exiled to Australia, who escaped by stealing the governor's boat. Despite his nostalgia for a free communism which never was, he confesses himself 'aboriginal' to Glasgow, that pioneer city of capitalist expansion.

The subjects closest to him, charged with life, are such phenomena as honeysuckle, 'mouse-people, wiry little snakes', mists, the blackbird which 'tweezers' worms and 'cocked a look at me/with his starboard eye' then 'rejected me/as being too much to swallow.'

He loves stones, whether solid individuals, or gathered into ancient circles; he salutes those animals he calls 'beautiful misfits', now extinct; and celebrates girls who smile at bus-stops; the soaring birds; 'the given coin of joy'; and the dark river of time.

In an elegy to his father he writes'.....throw/the dying on compost, my late father said;/and sure enough in season it will mingle/with the airy soil again, and make geraniums.'

That's his tone. His grandmother, too, has her place: 'I wanted to drink to her/but the pub was closed.'

His humour, honesty, affection and his ironic eye give us hope for the ordinary, and proves that poetry, despite everything, can rejoice.

Before Playing Romeo by Jane Weir
ISBN 978-0-9550023-8-0 review by Elspeth Brown

These poems are textural in design, sometimes sensual, a party of persona, lovers, paintings and edgy incident. This is a collection to return to aware of new aspects and looking for some elusive answer. The poems are inventive, teasing and often unsettling for the reader. Unsettling because in many of them the reader is deliberately made part of something yet ultimately excluded. Sometimes it is like reading someone else's letters. It is an effective device for making the reader curious but also to stand back. Nothing is as it seems.

In 'Stranmillis Room,' for example as in many of the love poems there are erotic elements yet a sadness of parting and insecurity. 'only the night tweaking dusk/and dusk does as it's told and drifts/in from the

Stranmillis entrance, /stippling sulphur yellow, pollen sprung/from wands of
pussy willow-/and questions like, *why do we keep doing this/to each other?* go
unanswered/...

Dusk and mist often herald uncertainty loss and love. 'Walking in
Fog to Riber ' 'They call it fog...this is a sign from you/ to say you've let
your hair/ down, for me to wander,/ comforted through./Deep greys
concentrate/in the park, gather intensely/in bold swirls beside/the river's
wavy parting.'

Many of the poems have an erotic teasing undertone but the textures
are so interconnected with no seams showing that it is hard to say where the
emotions change or overlap. She can make two people watching a pair of
ferrets sound lascivious. This is from 'With Matt staring at Ferrets.' 'Their
canines snaked/ like arm bangles, /chivvying upper lips, / and that
maddening tide, the ceaseless dock and cluck/of the chocolate mitt/ against
the belly of the cinnamon/and the tail teasing.'

There are variety of persona invoked in the poems, among them the
voice of Rizzio talking to Mary Queen of Scots. From 'Rizzio,' 'Mary, I
beseech you!/ Forgive me crumbling/ into crazy Piedimontese./ Don't stand
there gutting/Scots, dabbing with French your lips.../ Again we have some
of the intimacy and the sense of the outsider understanding some but not all
of their conversation.

Interviewed on Woman's Hour about her previous collection, Jane
Weir agreed that her background of Italian and English parentage, (she was
born in Salford to which she attributes a particular sense of humour) gives
her an insight into other people's territory. She feels that there are no such
areas as no go territory in poetry. You have to be able to shake things up.
This makes Before Playing Romeo a very interesting collection.

For the Hills I Sing by Pam Russell
ISBN 0-9554056-7-x/978-0-9554056-7-9 review by Elspeth Brown

This chapbook, and those in the two following reviews, is part of a
group by Women Poets of the Borders.

Pam Russell has a strong visual sense of place. In the best of her
poems she takes you to the countryside she observes with love. The poems I
enjoyed most are the ones where she is using her own voice in a direct way.
Occasionally I felt she lapsed into cliché as in 'a star filled canopy', from
'Moorland Song'. 'Paradise,' with its relaxed rhyme and rhythm. gets to the
heart of what makes wild countryside so exciting; it is not just observing, it
is identifying. 'With eagles I ride thermals/ with skylarks trill and sing, /
chase shadows on the hillside/..." She has an affinity for nature and skill in
sharing it.

My favourite poems in this collection are 'Fenland' and 'Fen Dusk'. With both these poems Pam Russell gives the impression of writing at the scene like a painter with an easel. The observation is detailed and here she uses repetition to intensify the pervasive nature of drizzle 'A dull damp day, /persistent drizzle, /pervasive damp': -the sibilant hiss of 'wisps of mist.'

Something in the Blood by Vivien Jones
ISBN 978-0-9554056-8-6 review by Elspeth Brown

Vivien ranges from poems of her childhood, her family and experiences of Italy in this collection. She looks beyond the small details to the universal significance. Several of her poems are involved in relationships where the poet or personae is controlling emotion that is nevertheless significant. In 'Isabella's Garden,' the Italian guide is professional with her information while the poet is deeply moved. 'The paintings are in the Louvre, /she said flatly quoting the guide book, / stealing a look at my flooding eyes.' This compares with 'Best Medicine.' An incident between mother and son, final stanza, 'Sometimes/the best expression of love/is two bacon rolls at midnight/ and no comment.' 'Chambers Street Museum' cleverly contrasts the energy of two small excited boys and the static displays. Vivien has an unique ability to balance the adult and child view from within her own psyche.

The controlled tension within 'Belated' is effective. 'These are things I never said/ from when we were so jealous' This is a very honest poem about a relationship and the dichotomy of love and jealousy. 'you thrashing me with your loveliness/me thrashing you with my intelligence/' Still some ambiguity, a backhander of a compliment. Taut emotion is still notable in the final lines, 'I did marry a teacher and, / since you're not around, /he does want me.'

'Milne Graden Poems' by Laurna Robertson
ISBN 978-0-9554056-9-3 review by Elspeth Brown

Laurna Robertson begins her collection with a poem about writing, 'At the Window.' Writers will identify with this waiting for the spark, the delicate ideas and words that become a poem,' like brittle leaves/whispering/under the gate/...like mouse tails/ quivering/between plant pots'. I particularly loved that mouse tail simile, it was so effective yet so other. Laurna combines sophistication and clarity with strong original imagery. 'Don't look into their eyes/ the Sorrow Sisters/ or they'll draw thick, dark lines /round your brightest memory.' (From 'Zero'.) Her subjects are varied. 'Archive Budapest', 'Homeland (Latvia),' both serious poems In 'Archive, Budapest' the nursery type style heightens the horror of the story of a husband who was shot. 'These are the threads/ beginning to fray, /where a young wife rubbed/ dark bloodstains away/'

The title for this chapbook comes from Laurna Robertson's move from Edinburgh to the eponymous Milne Graden. '…Milne Graden turns/ /on the slow drift of current, /on the skill in the ghillie's oar/on the weight in the angler's boots/'

This is a poet who made me connect to her subject and feel yes, I see it, this is how it is.

Earth. Fire, Air and Water* by Robert Marsland Ettrick Forest Press ISBN 978-1-873586-43-3 £6.99 review by John Hudson

In the covering letter that came with this volume, Ettrick Forest Press states that it "intends to be Scotland's leading poetry publisher in five year's time". This bold and, possibly, vainglorious claim is similarly reflected in Marsland's poetry which is trying too hard. I am not saying that there isn't talent here – I am not sure – but read on the page there is much material that the poet might have axed. I can imagine some of the works, such as "Wankered" on page 10 would perform well in an open mike session down the pub but a little lingering leaves this reader tired of the bombast, inaccuracy and average technical skill. Worse is the pretension. The writer fails to distinguish between the feelings and reaction induced by art, such as classical music, and their expression, and phrases such as "Brahms took things as seriously as I" ("Thankyou" [sic] page 40) seems to elevate the poet's thoughts and feelings beyond their station. I will leave the reader to decide who is the greater artist, the serious Hamburger or Robert Marsland.

Title as printed, including full-stop after Earth

Waves 2007, The Society of Civil and Public Service Writers' Poetry Workshop Anthology. Contact Liz Rowlands – pw@gothicgarden.freeserve.co.uk review by John Hudson

This came to Markings through the BDS Literature in Libraries initiative and it is worthwhile bringing it to our readers' attention because the Society's activities are quite extensive, including publications, workshops and meetings. Membership is open to anyone who works or has worked in the Civil or Public Service or who has served in the Armed Forces.

The volume, modestly produced and containing 28 pages, is typical of such an anthology, a bit of a pick and mix, where everyone finds something they like and something that they don't. However, all the contributions are intelligent and contributors show an awareness of language and craft with a broad cultural frame of reference. I liked Derek Adams "Automatons", reflections on automatic writing dear to the surrealists; I also noticed Norman Bisset whose work has previously appeared in Markings.

With a broader membership and higher productions standards this could become a fascinating niche production.

And in here, the Menagerie by Angela Cleland Templar Poetry
ISBN 978-0-955002-39-7 £9.99 (hardback) review by John Hudson

Angela Cleland is a poet who writes with energy and vivid imagery. Her use of language is natural and while the technical range is limited she also avoids most of the pitfalls that poets, even some well-established, fall into – there is little obscurity disguising emptiness however there is some fanciful posturing. There are poems that come across as exercises and there is a tendency for the poet to imagine herself in the skin of other animate or inanimate objects. These poems raise a shrug of the shoulders and a "why" reaction. As if it weren't far too formulaic and fashionable to imagine oneself as a mouse or a wristwatch, one also has to have something to say. To be fair, she does have something to say – the wristwatch is a metaphor for growing indifference in a relationship over time but there is a feeling of lack of substance, as if the very exercise is making the poem longer than it need be to make the point. These hangovers from writers' group exercises and the legacy of Ted Hughes apart, Angela Cleland is a poet from whom I hope we have much more to read.

On the flyleaf, Ken Cockburn Luath Press
ISBN 978-1-906307-18-9 £7.99 review by John Hudson

Ken Cockburn is becoming a better, more accomplished and wider-ranging poet with every volume he publishes. His fascination for taking incidental detail that reveals a deeper truth is just as apparent here as in his earlier work but there is a greater technical range and, in places, a new lyricism which offsets the sometimes demanding nature of his intellect. On the flyleaf presents poems that you can simply enjoy and those that are more demanding (a fair share of the volume) make you want to burrow down into the references to reveal resonances that open up fresh views onto the physical, psychological and intellectual world around us. Always happy to experiment but never fatuously so, Cockburn's work loves languages and the geographical space they occupy in the world and in the mind. Shifting in and out of French and German, alluding to Goethe or Ovid, any sense of pretentiousness is quickly offset by the poet's personal transparency and intellectual rigour.

Dear Alice – Narratives of Madness by Tom Pow Salt Publishing
ISBN 978-1-84471-416-2 review by JB Pick

Tom Pow is used to journeys, but this one is dark, troubling and close
to home. He teaches now at the University Campus known as the Crichton
in Dumfries. It is a dignified set of buildings in a spacious park, but for
more than a hundred years the Crichton was a lunatic asylum, run on the
most modern and progressive lines known to the mid-Nineteenth Century.

It is said that Dr. Browne, the first Superintendent, 'is master of a
system in which incessant watchfulness is exercised to arrest and destroy in
their birth the vicious practices and eccentricities of the insane.' A poem
comments; 'From secret hidey-holes we watch/ them hopelessly embracing/
their own exile'.

This is a regime and atmosphere in which a poet can walk safely only
with perfect balance and a multi-layered sensibility, always aware of the
damaged and powerful ghosts which surround him.

In Tom Pow's poems realism and imagination work together. The
first poem, 'Inauguration' conjures up the birth of the University campus,
at which the criminally insane crowd the hall, followed by the dead, who
'mooch in, lifting their heavy lids to the light.' The poet comments, 'We are
a *Liberal* Arts College after all.' 'a sound of thunder fills the air/ and the
fountains/ start to shake'.

Behind the voices of observers, witnesses, inmates, wardens, and the
stark or tender stories, it is the poet's own voice which finds exact words to
let in light.

A girl, blind at birth, "crouches by the window/ endeavouring (it is
said) to seek out the fugitive light/as it enters the broken pane."

The phrase 'it is said' seems to hold here a whole cargo of perceptions.

In a description of a watercolour in the asylum we contemplate "On a
green grassy sea, the islanders wait./ Soon the light will leave these three
frozen figures:/ each a prisoner in his own black dock."

Grim irony enters when inmate Angus McKay smashes furniture,
shrieks, howls like an owl: "though this last/ does not appear/ in his case
notes from Bedlam –/ 'hooting and howling' in southern parts/ being
thought not/ abnormal for a Scot".

There is exact insight in this vision of a woman who rescues five seeds
from an apple: 'She sang to them/ of apples on a summer day/ shining in
sunlight. She stroked/ the tiny back of each one/ as it sat like a little dark
flame/ on her finger tips'.

While enduring a lecture: "Someone in the shadow sniffs/ '*Materiality
my arse*' –/ Where words fail, I'll never follow."

Tom Pow's words do not fail. We follow him through this place of
living shadows and experience light.

Driving Home

The evening is barely audible
with low-key cloud and trees
composing their leaves in
what little light is left.

Young roe deer tiptoe over the back road,
disappear into woods,
indistinguishable
from the flash of birch bark.

Somewhere in the curling grass you, maybe,
watch me watching the ducks
hang and hang above the bridge
like old wall ornaments.

You sing in me what I can't understand
so I drive home in silence
waiting for the penny to drop,
for the moon to clear the cloud.

Sacred

The road to the well's due east. OK. Lit
low, walking the afternoon light now, down the hill,
up again, switchback, pond below, blond banners –

nothing but pleasant, this and us, thus; outspread
red campion and meadowsweet on a like late
weekend break with their latin in the hedge flanks,
blue clouds – OK. And now converging wood,
warm gate set with lichen. We fall in, skirt a soft
edging till the dark path at the elbow, sodden ground –

When I found the place last time I left something,
something, feather or flowers – a coin? – lip-service, cardboard,
2D, cheap play, little pool with no one at home, deep
brown unsure like lazy smoke. This time I drank.

OK. Stirring dregs, dust. Stirred? Stirring what slow – wishes? –
smoke, in any of us? More separate than stars as we fit
the photo joking among birch trees, bramble and ferns.

Libby Houston will be reading at The Bakehouse on August 2

Winter Evening

We are walking, just walking,
breathing and being, talked out,
crunching frost that hasn't succumbed
to day, that's lain like a sleeper
in a lover's still bed.

We have talked of love as long
as decades, beyond the passion
that makes mad, beyond lust
and unringing telephones,
the kind that's just muscle and skin,
air and honesty.

The words tasted of orange flesh
and bone white. So I stop now,
point silently to the lowering sky,
at the moon shining palely
through the ribs of the trees.
Your fingers find mine,
breath hangs crystals on the kind air.

Coming Home

You lie there reading in our bed
light of evening round your head
as I drive under evening skies
familiar beloved.

You lie there sleeping in our bed
the stars of midnight round your head
dark the sky as I lie down by my
familiar beloved.

You lie there smiling in our bed
yesterday's dreams inside your head
and as I dream I dream
familiar beloved.

You lie here waking in our bed
morning light around your head
as I move your body moves
familiar beloved.

You lie there darling in our bed
avenues of day inside your head
where we will walk, laugh, quarrel, talk
familiar beloved.

Delius's Amanuensis

What was the man's name - only a lad
to start with - who wrote down what
Delius played out of his head?

"Something on these lines" says Delius,
vague to start with, else what had
Fred - some name like that - got to do?

Did John walk round on his own, along
the streets of Paris, the promenade
at Southport, adding his ha'porth?

And those first nights, did Paul also
wear a black tie, standing to one side
caught up in the applause?

What did Jim do, after the real
Fred (Delius, Frederick) had gone
to heaven with his last sound?

Did the lad, a man now, look back like
a widower living on in a house where
the records can only wear out?

Or did he find his own private name -
the one I can't remember - and take up,
wiser now, wherever he'd left off?

Notes: a ruminative pause before each of the trial names;
Delius's amanuensis was called Eric Fenby.

Give a Snake a Bad Name

Summer so idyllic,
you'd almost expect to hear
strains of Delius drifting through
Surrey woodlands. Late afternoon
a fenced-off, quiet plantation,
cool shadows, but on a warm grass bank
a basking viper coiled in sleep.

It lay like a colour plate,
head signed with inverted vee,
settled on the body, wound in a spiral,
rope-thick, olive-grey,
its length patterned with a black zigzag,
the tail's contrasting orange tip,
a silent warning to steer clear.

Need to look closer drove me
to fork the reptile with a stick.
Outraged, it threshed and writhed,
hissing steam enough to scald.
Stepping back, I raised the stick,
but too quick, it serpentined away
under the sandy scrub.

After the apples were eaten,
the subtle snake's been given
a diabolical press,
cursed above cattle
to go on its belly and eat dust,
with judgement promised of bruises
to heels and heads, but not this time.

Camargue

Now at the day's expiring
Night's shawl drawn over the flagstones
These two sitting together
Easeful under plane trees
Assume the hues of dusk:
That last reluctant light
Dappling down time's cheek
Stealing over the hunched spent shoulders.

This – the Camargue
Where old men pass hushed evenings
Chancing a dice across a checkerboard
Their hands tremulous with age
And the uncertainties of dalliance
With this darting violet light.

Conversation hangs about them, soundless:
All is certain, all understood, no call for talk,
While small philosophies churr by on insect wings
All truth rising heavenward
In a spiral of pipe-smoke.

GAIL KELLY

Scots Pine

Tides

Mind and arm are matched to perfection;
the dipping sweep of our paddle blades,
rhythmic grace of their dip and pull
countering the next wave and the next;
and still
the round island seems to
recede from our prow.

Salt-stung faces become masks, and night
exhausts us. The canoe begins to fill
with rain, becomes heavier and ever
harder to paddle. We stop, flop forward
over our knees, or slump back,
in a blink asleep.

Made curious by our frantic labours
the giant turtle, our gleaming island,
returns and raises her lizard head
to look us over. Being neither shark nor
jellyfish, we are of no interest to her.

Belief

Wavelets lap at the canoe's thin sides
and, splash by trickle, continue
to fill it. Unsheltered, rocking afloat,
our skin shrivels from salt and sun.

Dozing, not one of us remarks on
the pre-sunset sky of ragged gold,
nor the hard, indifferent glitter
of the stars. We each awake spitting
alone in dawn's grey water, still
holding on to each our own paddle.

In the miles of ocean below we know
beasts of the deep are passing by, and
we each believe that — for the moment —
they are sated on all the recent carnage.

THE BAKEHOUSE

The Bakehouse & Markings Magazine
Programme of Events
May to December 2008

May 24th   **Laughing in the Dark**
The extraordinary story of a holocaust ventriloquist
A new play by Graeme Messer

June 11th & 12th   **Romeo and Juliet performed by Shakespeare's Globe**
in the grounds of the Crichton @ Dumfries
Sponsored by BDS & the Crichton Development Company

June 28th   **Tom Leonard - poetry**
One of Scotland's foremost and most radical
and respected poets

August 2nd   **Libby Houston - poetry**
Houston's poetry walks an exhilarating high wire
– Judith Kazantzis
plus
An Exhibition of Pictures & Words by Hugh Bryden
Preview 6.00pm, The Bakehouse Gallery

August 23rd   **Launch of Greedy for Mulberries**
Chrys Salt's Poetry Collection

September 27th   **Katrina Porteous - poetry**
Winner of a Gregory Award
and an Arts Foundation Award

November 8th   **Hugh McMillan & Launch of Markings 27**
A nationally established poet launches
a nationally established magazine

December 6th   **Gerry Cambridge – poetry and music**
Poet, photographer, musician, editor and critic

Performances start 7.30pm
Tickets £7.50 (£6.00 concs)*
44 High Street, Gatehouse of Fleet, DG7 2HP
01557 814175 bookings@thebakehouse.info
*with the exception of Romeo and Juliet (see back cover advertisement)